ISBN 978-1-5279-8194-2
PIBN 10927167

1 MONTH OF
FREE
READING

at

www.ForgottenBooks.com

By purchasing this book you are eligible for one month membership to ForgottenBooks.com, giving you unlimited access to our entire collection of over 1,000,000 titles via our web site and mobile apps.

To claim your free month visit: www.forgottenbooks.com/free927167

English
Français
Deutsche
Italiano
Español
Português

www.forgottenbooks.com

Mythology Photography **Fiction**
Fishing Christianity **Art** Cooking
Essays Buddhism Freemasonry
Medicine **Biology** Music **Ancient
Egypt** Evolution Carpentry Physics
Dance Geology **Mathematics** Fitness
Shakespeare **Folklore** Yoga Marketing
Confidence Immortality Biographies
Poetry **Psychology** Witchcraft
Electronics Chemistry History **Law**
Accounting **Philosophy** Anthropology
Alchemy Drama Quantum Mechanics
Atheism Sexual Health **Ancient History**
Entrepreneurship Languages Sport
Paleontology Needlework Islam
Metaphysics Investment Archaeology
Parenting Statistics Criminology
Motivational

PROGRAMS OF
GUIDANCE

BULLETIN, 1932, No. 17

✦

MONOGRAPH No. 14

WILLIAM JOHN COOPER, *United States Commissioner of Education, Director.*
LEONARD V. KOOS, *Professor of Secondary Education, The University of Chicag
Associate Director.*
CARL A. JESSEN, *Specialist in Secondary Education, United States Office of Educatio
Coordinator.*

BOARD OF CONSULTANTS

MONOGRAPHS

1. Summary. Leonard V. Koos and Staff. 15 cents.
2. The Horizontal Organization of Secondary Education—A Comparison of Co
   prehensive and Specialized Schools. Grayson N. Kefauver, Victor H. No
   and C. Elwood Drake. 20 cents.
3. Part-Time Secondary Schools. Grayson N. Kefauver, Victor H. Noll, and
   Elwood Drake. 10 cents.
4. The Secondary-School Population. Grayson N. Kefauver, Victor H. Noll,
   C. Elwood Drake. 10 cents.
5. The Reorganization of Secondary Education. Francis T. Spaulding, O. I. Fre
   erick, and Leonard V. Koos. 40 cents.
6. The Smaller Secondary Schools. Emery N. Ferriss, W. H. Gaumnitz, and P. Ro
   Brammell. 15 cents.
7. Secondary Education for Negroes. Ambrose Caliver. 10 cents.
8. District Organization and Secondary Education. Fred Engelhardt, William
   Zeigel, jr., William M. Proctor, and Scovel S. Mayo. 15 cents.
9. Legal and Regulatory Provisions Affecting Secondary Education. Ward
   Keesecker and Franklin C. Sewell. 10 cents.
10. Articulation of High School and College. P. Roy Brammell. 10 cents.
11. Administration and Supervision. Fred Engelhardt, William H. Zeigel, jr., an
    Roy O. Billett. 15 cents.
12. Selection and Appointment of Teachers. W. S. Deffenbaugh and William
    Zeigel, jr. 10 cents.
13. Provisions for Individual Differences, Marking, and Promotion. Roy O. Billet
    40 cents.
14. Programs of Guidance. William C. Reavis. 10 cents.
15. Research in Secondary Schools. William H. Zeigel, jr. 10 cents.
16. Interpreting the Secondary School to the Public. Belmont Farley. 10 cents.
17. The Secondary-School Library. B. Lamar Johnson. 10 cents.
18. Procedures in Curriculum Making. Edwin S. Lide. 10 cents.
19. The Program of Studies. A. K. Loomis, Edwin S. Lide, and B. Lamar Johnso
    15 cents.
20. Instruction in English. Dora V. Smith. 10 cents.
21. Instruction in the Social Studies. William G. Kimmel. 10 cents.
22. Instruction in Science. Wilbur L. Beauchamp. 10 cents.
23. Instruction in Mathematics. Edwin S. Lide. 10 cents.
24. Instruction in Foreign Languages. Helen M. Eddy. 10 cents.
25. Instruction in Music and Art. Anne E. Pierce and Robert S. Hilpert. 10 cent
26. Nonathletic Extracurriculum Activities. William C. Reavis and George E. V
    Dyke. 15 cents.
27. Intramural and Interscholastic Athletics. P. Roy Brammell. 10 cents.
28. Health and Physical Education. P. Roy Brammell. 10 cents.

[Silhouette on cover by WALTER J. GREENLEAF]

UNITED STATES DEPARTMENT OF THE INTERIOR
HAROLD L. ICKES : SECRETARY

OFFICE OF EDUCATION : WILLIAM JOHN COOPER
COMMISSIONER

PROGRAMS
OF GUIDANCE

BY

WILLIAM C. REAVIS

BULLETIN, 1932, NO. 17

NATIONAL SURVEY OF SECONDARY EDUCATION

MONOGRAPH NO. 14

UNITED STATES
GOVERNMENT PRINTING OFFICE
WASHINGTON : 1933

NOTE

William C. Reavis, the author of this monograph, is professor of education at the University of Chicago and specialist in secondary school administration of the NATIONAL SURVEY OF SECONDARY EDUCATION. *William John Cooper, United States Commissioner of Education, is director of the Survey; Leonard V. Koos, professor of secondary education at the University of Chicago, is associate director; and Carl A. Jessen, specialist in secondary education of the Office of Education, is coordinator.*

[II]

CONTENTS

LETTER OF TRANSMITTAL

DEPARTMENT OF THE INTERIOR,
OFFICE OF EDUCATION,
Washington, D. C., May, 1933.

SIR: Within a period of 30 years the high-school enrollment has increased from a little over 10 per cent of the population of high-school age to more than 50 per cent of that population. This enrollment is so unusual for a secondary school that it has attracted the attention of Europe, where only 8 to 10 per cent attend secondary schools. Many European educators have said that we are educating too many people. I believe, however, that the people of the United States are now getting a new conception of education. They are coming to look upon education as a preparation for citizenship and for daily life rather than for the money return which comes from it. They are looking upon the high school as a place for their boys and girls to profit at a period when they are not yet acceptable to industry.

In order that we may know where we stand in secondary education, the membership of the North Central Association of Colleges and Secondary Schools four years ago took the lead in urging a study. It seemed to them that it was wise for such a study to be made by the Government of the United States rather than by a private foundation, for if such an agency studied secondary education it might be accused, either rightly or wrongly, of a bias toward a special interest. When the members of a committee of this association appeared before the Bureau of the Budget in 1928, they received a very courteous hearing. It was impossible, so the Chief of the Budget Bureau thought, to obtain all the money which the commission felt desirable; with the money which was obtained, $225,000, to be expended over a 3-year period, it was found impossible to do all the things that the committee had in mind. It was possible, however, to study those things which pertained strictly to secondary education; that is, its organization; its curriculum, including some of the more fundamental subjects, and particularly those subjects on which a comparison could be made between the present and earlier periods; its extracurriculum, which is almost entirely new in the past 30 years; the pupil population; and administrative and supervisory problems, personnel, and activities.

The handling of this Survey was intrusted to Dr. Leonard V. Koos, of the University of Chicago. With great skill he has, working on a full-time basis during his free quarters from the University of Chicago and part time during other quarters, brought it to a conclusion.

This manuscript was prepared by Dr. William C. Reavis, of the University of Chicago, who was employed on the study on part-time basis. After a careful study of guidance service he undertook to visit the more important places where good guidance programs were in effect. Ten places are picked out for description in this monograph including some 4 township high schools in the State of Illinois. In addition to these there will be found a description of the guidance work in the five cities of Boston, Chicago, Providence, Cincinnati, Milwaukee, and in the independent Milwaukee Vocational School.

The educational and vocational guidance given in individual high schools in each of these cities is described fully. In some places the service has been attached to the city government. In other places it was from the beginning more closely connected to the school system. There is generally a marked tendency for it to be found in the schools. In some of these schools there seems to be no distinction made between the work in administration and the functions in guidance. For instance, they are closely connected in the New Trier Township High School. In the Joliet Township High School, on the other hand, they are clearly differentiated. The last chapter summarizes four main types of guidance activities and describes guidance in a small rural school in California. The conclusion is that guidance may exist in schools of any size if its necessity is fully understood by the principal and faculty of the school.

I recommend the publication of this manuscript as part of the National Survey of Secondary Education.

Respectfully,

WM. JOHN COOPER,
Commissioner.

The SECRETARY OF THE INTERIOR.

PROGRAMS OF GUIDANCE

CHAPTER I : THE NEED, STATUS, AND MEANING
OF GUIDANCE

The need of guidance in secondary schools.—Guidance services on the part of the secondary school are rendered necessary by at least four conditions, namely: (1) The character of the demands for modern secondary education, (2) the changes in the social and economic order to which the secondary-school pupil must adjust himself, (3) the needs of the adolescent for counsel and guidance, and (4) the necessity of avoiding waste in the process of education.

Demand for modern secondary education.—The secondary school of a generation ago had a narrow curriculum, designed chiefly to prepare young people for college. The decision to send or not to send a youth to high school was at that time usually made by the family. The individual who presented himself for admission to a secondary school generally knew what he was seeking. After admission the individual was primarily responsible for his own failure or success. He knew in advance the nature of the opportunities offered by the school and successful accomplishment on his part was assumed. If he failed to meet the requirements of the school, he either tried again or voluntarily withdrew. It was taken for granted by the individual that the family sacrifice should not be made in vain and that the secondary school was not maintained for those who could not profit from the academic opportunities provided.

To-day the situation described in the preceding paragraph has been greatly changed. In most States pupils are required to attend school until 15, 16, or 17 years of age. In many communities public sentiment for secondary education is so strong that virtually all children under 18 years of age are enrolled in the secondary school. As a result the school has had to make marked changes in organization in an attempt to meet the needs of its varied personnel. Instead of a required curriculum designed to prepare chiefly for admission to college, many curriculums are now offered from which the pupils may select. The extent of the change is shown by Van Dyke [1] in a comparative study of the curriculums of 35 secondary schools for the periods 1906–1911 and 1929–1930. In the first period, 53 different courses were offered in all the subject fields, a total of 828 courses and an average of 23.7 courses to a school; in the second period, 306 different courses were offered, a total of 1,683 courses and an average of 48.1 to a school. The expansion and enrichment of the program of studies in this period of approximately 25 years can not be explained solely on the ground of increased enrollment, for the population of the school districts studied increased only 66.5 per cent in the period, while the number of different courses increased 477 per cent. The increase in course offerings represents an effort on the part of the secondary schools to meet the various needs of their pupil personnel.

Changes in the economic and social order.—The adjustment of pupils of high-school age to the complex world in which they live is no simple matter. The individual's world to-day is vastly larger and more complex than it was a generation ago. Important changes in the social and economic structure render both social and vocational adjustments difficult. The rapid shifting of population from rural to urban life has complicated the processes of social and economic adjustment. As a result, the individual at the threshold of his entrance into college or industry and adult community life is frequently overwhelmed by experiences which he does not fully understand and can not clearly interpret. Since the home is usually unable to provide the guidance needed in the interpretation of many experiences encountered by the youth, the secondary school is compelled to assume a portion of the function formerly discharged by the home. If the school fails to assume this function, the individual is apt to flounder for want of guidance and may fail to find himself with respect to his interests and capacity or to take full advantage

---

[1] Van Dyke, G. E. Trends in the Development of the High-School Offerings, II. School Review, 39 : 738, December 1931.

of the opportunities offered in school and society for his growth and development.

The needs of adolescents for guidance.—The needs of the youth of high-school age for guidance are both many and varied.. On account of the stage in his development, physical, mental, and social changes may occur which baffle his understanding. The high-school age is commonly regarded as a period of great importance in the life of the youth because of the adjustments which must be made. Problems that have to do with the intellectual and physical development, choice of companions, social activities, and the formation of right social attitudes must be met and solved. The school is required to understand the needs of its young people and to provide the guidance service which the pupils as individuals require.

Waste in the processes of secondary education.—That many schools have not met successfully the responsibilities imposed by the guidance function is evidenced by high percentages of withdrawal in each succeeding year of the secondary school and by high percentages of failure in different subject-matter fields. Recent evidence of withdrawals in secondary schools is furnished in the survey [2] of public schools of Chicago, Ill., in which the remarkable holding power of 98 per cent was found for the ninth grade. The percentage drops to 78 for the tenth grade, 49 for the eleventh, and 34 for the twelfth. For the same secondary schools the percentage of pupils failing in their work for the semester ending January, 1931, was 12, and June, 1931, 11.1. The range of the different schools for the semester ending June, 1931, was from 6.4 per cent to 17.5. Data concerning failures in secondary schools elsewhere reveal percentages both greater and less than those cited for Chicago. However, irrespective of amount, failure involves waste in the process of secondary education which can and should be reduced and as far as possible prevented through the effective guidance of pupils.

Status of guidance in secondary schools.—Data collected in 1927 [3] from a sample group of 522 secondary schools in 41 States ranging in enrollment from 4 pupils to 6,500 show that,

[2] Strayer, G. D. Report of the Survey of the Schools of Chicago, Ill., 1932. Secondary Education in Chicago, Vol. II, p. 149.

[3] Reavis, W. C., *and* Woellner, R. C. Office Practices in Secondary Schools, pp. 190–197. Chicago, Laidlaw Bros., 1930.

according to the judgment of the principals, educational guidance was provided in 87 per cent of the schools, personal guidance in 83 per cent of the schools, and vocational guidance in 74 per cent of the schools. The findings of the sampling indicate that the activities involved in the three general types of guidance specified are carried on in the large majority of secondary schools. The small schools enrolling 100 pupils and fewer give considerably less attention to educational and vocational guidance than the schools in the larger enrollment groups, which vary only slightly in the relative

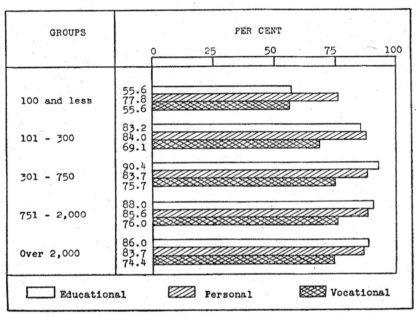

FIGURE 1.—Percentages of schools in different enrollment groups offering educational, personal, and vocational guidance

emphasis given to the three types. The data show that for schools of all sizes vocational guidance receives somewhat less attention than educational and personal guidance. (Fig. 1.)

Other data [4] collected regarding specific phases of guidance during the same year from 336 secondary schools in 44 States ranging in enrollment from 47 to 4,072 show that a median of 24.9 activities in guidance with a range of 51 activities (5 to 56) were reported by the principals to be carried on in their

---

[4] Koos, Leonard V., and Kefauver, Grayson N. Guidance in Secondary Schools, pp. 511–513 New York, The Macmillan Co., 1932.

schools. Among the leading activities through which guidance opportunities were provided in the different schools were discipline in 72.2 per cent of the schools; oversight of conduct, 74.6 per cent; guidance concerning quality of work, 63.5 per cent; curriculum guidance, 60.8 per cent; vocational guidance, 37.7 per cent; placement, 20.4 per cent; and follow-up service, 13.5 per cent.

The variation in the percentages of the two investigations cited is accounted for in part by the vagueness of the term "guidance." To some persons the term "guidance" is very general and is virtually synonymous with the process of education. An individual with this conception might consider that curriculum guidance is educational, personal, and vocational in character when evaluating guidance activities according to the three general categories, but as curriculum guidance only and not vocational or personal when evaluating guidance according to specific categories.

The diverse meaning of the term "guidance."—The foregoing facts indicate that guidance in some form or other (general or specific) is a well-established function in most secondary schools. The activities carried on in secondary schools under the caption are, however, extremely varied. In some schools guidance probably means whatever principal or teachers do for pupils in the way of personal council or advice. In other schools guidance activities are roughly differentiated into types, such as educational, personal, vocational, social, moral, and the like. Still other schools analyze guidance into specific activities, such as providing assistance to pupils in choosing curriculums, overcoming deficiencies, developing special talents, and cultivating intellectual interests, or imparting occupational information, advising regarding the choice of an occupation, assisting in securing employment, helping in the choice of a college, and giving supervisory oversight to an individual after employment.

Both general and specific activities of the sort enumerated in the foregoing paragraph are evidently carried on in many secondary schools. In some schools the activities are carried on only informally and incidentally by the regular school officers—principal, deans, and teachers. In other schools they are carried on formally and systematically under the direction of persons specially selected for the purpose and definitely charged with the responsibility of serving pupils through the types of specific activities enumerated.

Scope of this monograph.—This monograph deals with guidance programs in secondary schools. The nature, status, and meaning of guidance have been presented. Consideration is given in Chapter II to the guidance functionaries found in sample groups of secondary schools, and in Chapter III to the more important guidance activities observed in the schools visited by the author of this monograph. The treatment of functionaries and activities in Chapters II and III is introduced to provide the background for the case reports on guidance programs presented in the subsequent chapters. Case reports of five school systems and five individual schools reputed to have outstanding programs of guidance are presented in Chapters IV to XIII. All of these, except one,[5] were visited by the author, who observed the workings of the guidance programs and conferred with the guidance functionaries. Other school systems and individual schools with innovating programs of guidance were also visited, but case reports of these are not included because of limitation of space and the fact that the reports presented are believed to be adequately representative, although they can not be assumed to include anything like all the outstanding programs of guidance in the country. The greater number of reports on programs in the Mid-West is explained by their proximity to the base of operations of the investigator.

Chapter XIV contains an overview of the guidance programs presented in Chapters IV to XIII and a supplementary analysis of a guidance program in a small secondary school as described by Proctor.[6] Small secondary schools were not studied in the present investigation, for the reason that they are the subject of special inquiry reported in Monograph No. 6.[7] Chapter IX of Monograph No. 6 includes description of guidance practices in a number of small schools as a group and also cites unusual practices in several individual schools.

---

[5] This school was visited and reported by G. E. Van Dyke, who also prepared the reports for two other schools.

[6] Proctor, W. M. Guidance Program of a Rural High School in California. Junior-Senior High School Clearing House, 5: 14–16, September 1930.

[7] Ferriss, Emery N., Gaumnitz, W. H., *and* Brammell, P. Roy. The Smaller Secondary Schools. National Survey of Secondary Education. Office of Education Bulletin, 1932, No. 17, Monograph No. 6. Washington, D.C., Government Printing Office.

CHAPTER II : GUIDANCE FUNCTIONARIES IN SECONDARY SCHOOLS

The guidance functionaries found.—The functionary found responsible most frequently for the assumption of guidance duties in a sampling of 522 schools [1] is the school principal. In 77 per cent of the schools this officer provides guidance for boys and in 56 per cent for girls. The assistant principals are assigned the responsibility for boys in 32 per cent of the schools and for girls in 26 per cent. Counselors for boys and deans for girls are employed for the purpose in 21 and 50 per cent of the schools, respectively. The guidance functions are delegated to other officers whose titles were not specified in approximately one-sixth of the schools.

Other data [2] of a more specific character reveal a tendency in secondary schools to develop programs of counseling and guidance around different guidance functionaries. (Fig. 2.) The data show that guidance activities of some sort are carried on in the large majority of schools, both small and large. The principal is the most prevalent guidance officer found in the small schools and the home-room adviser, dean of girls, and dean of boys in the large schools. However, a noticeable difference in the extent of use of the specialist in counseling, namely, the counselor, is observed in the large schools when compared with the small schools (28 per cent as compared to 2.7 per cent).

The principal as a guidance functionary.—The principal is chiefly responsible for the guidance activities in the majority of the schools with enrollments of fewer than 200. His different relations to the guidance program are revealed by the data [3] presented in Figure 3. The findings show that he personally carries on guidance work for all the pupils in approximately two-thirds of the small schools. That

---

[1] Reavis, W. C., *and* Woellner, R. C., op. cit., pp. 191–197.

[2] Koos, Leonard V., *and* Kefauver, Grayson N., op. cit., pp. 515–517.

[3] Ibid., pp. 578–581.

guidance organizations are lacking in the majority of the schools with enrollments of fewer than 200 is shown by the facts (1) that the principal heads the guidance work or serves as one of a group of advisers in only a few schools (8.1 per cent), (2) that he acts as chairman of the guidance committee in only 5.4 per cent of the schools, and (3) that he is responsible for developing home-room programs in only 10.8 per cent of the schools. In some of the schools (29.7 per cent) he serves either as adviser of boys or assumes advisory responsibility with boys as one of the guidance duties which he

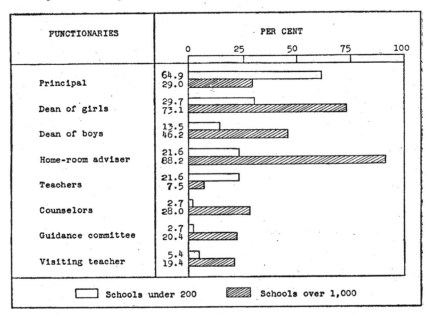

FIGURE 2.—Percentages of functionaries specified as performing guidance duties in schools with enrollments of fewer than 200 and more than 1,000

personally performs. He reports recommending pupils to college in about half the schools, and making studies to improve the basis of guidance in about a tenth of the schools. The work of the principal as a guidance functionary in the schools with enrollments of fewer than 200 is obviously very general in character, and probably belongs more properly in the field of administration than in guidance.

In the schools with enrollments in excess of 1,000 the relations of the principal to the guidance program vary from the practices found in the smaller schools in the following

respects: In approximately two-thirds of the schools he heads
the work in a general way, a fact which suggests the more
frequent existence of guidance organizations in the larger
schools. He serves as one of a group of advisers, as chairman,
and as member of a guidance committee, and is responsible
for developing the home-room program in a larger percentage
of the schools enrolling more than 1,000 than in those enrolling
fewer than 200. On the contrary, the principals of the
larger schools personally carry on the guidance work and
serve as advisers of the boys much less frequently than in the

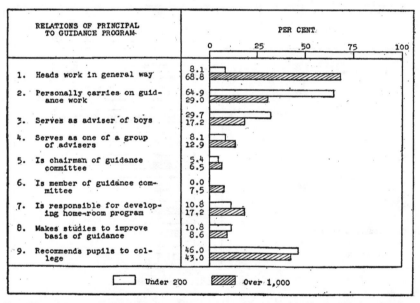

FIGURE 3.—Percentages of guidance duties specified which were performed by principals in
schools of fewer than 200 and more than 1,000

smaller schools. In making studies designed to improve the
basis of the guidance work and in recommending pupils to
college the percentages of frequency for the two types of
schools are about the same.

In the schools which develop their guidance programs
around general administrative officers, guidance activities are
often subordinated to other administrative duties. Furthermore, in dealing both with individuals and with groups the
administrative officer is sometimes inhibited in the performance of a guidance activity by the urgency of prior

[9]

performance of some nonguidance administrative activity. In practice administration may interfere with guidance and guidancy may interfere with administration. This relation often renders guidance difficult by officers whose primary responsibility is administration.

The dean of girls and dean of boys as guidance functionaries.— In recent years, especially in large secondary schools, the principal has utilized the services of the dean of girls and the dean of boys in the administration of the pupil personnel. These officers generally teach part time, devoting the re-

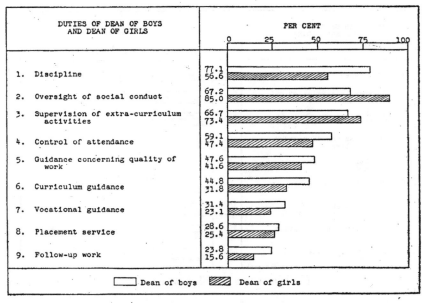

FIGURE 4.—Percentages of duties specified which were performed by the dean of boys and the dean of girls in 336 secondary schools

maining time to the specific personnel duties assigned. In some of the large schools they devote full time to personnel duties.[4]

Analysis of the duties [5] of these officers (Fig. 4) shows that their four chief functions are administrative in character. Five important duties fall more clearly within the field of guidance, but these duties are performed less frequently than the administrative duties. The dean of boys is charged

[4] Reavis, W. C., *and* Woellner, R. C., op. cit., p. 43.
[5] Koos, Leonard V., *and* Kefauver, Grayson N., op. cit., p. 534.

with guidance duties to a greater extent than the dean of girls. The data show the deans have been utilized by the principals of secondary schools in the capacity of administrative officers to a greater extent than in the capacity of counselors.

Home-room advisers as guidance functionaries.—In many schools the home room is utilized as the unit of the guidance program. This is especially true of the larger secondary schools in which the home room may have previously existed as a unit for carrying on certain routine administrative activities. Approximately seven-eighths of the schools studied by Koos and Kefauver with enrollments in excess of 1,000 employed the home-room organization in the development of guidance programs. Since the same investigators found that home rooms were utilized in only one-fifth of the schools enrolling fewer than 200 pupils, the conclusion is warranted that the home-room organization is characteristic of the larger secondary schools.

The home room is usually organized as the school home of a group of pupils whether the group be small or large. Usually it is required to care for from 30 to 40 pupils, although in some school systems large assembly rooms make possible the organization of the school into "houses" or home rooms with from 200 to 400 members.

The home-room plan of organization makes possible the segregation of pupils in groups under the leadership of a regular teacher whose responsibility for the home-room group is sponsorship rather than instruction. The plan enables the sponsor and pupils to establish cooperative relations as a means of realizing the purposes for which the type of organization exists. Whether the home-room group remains with the adviser for a semester, term, or during the membership of the group in the school does not matter greatly, provided the purposes of the organization are clearly conceived.

Broadly speaking, the chief purpose of the home room is guidance, and the specific activities carried on in it should come largely under that category. To this end it should be organized as a guidance laboratory and not as another classroom. The atmosphere of the room should be democratic and should be conducive to self-discovery and self-revelation. To serve the members of the home-room group the adviser must know them as individuals and as members of a primary group.

The mere organization of a school for guidance purposes into home-room groups does not guarantee that guidance activities will be better performed by home-room advisers than by administrative officers. Unless home-room advisers are trained for guidance work their activities will very likely resemble either the activities of the teacher or of the minor administrative officer. It is difficult to indicate to what extent training has been provided for home-room advisers in schools that have adopted the home-room plan as a guidance program. Data from the sampling of 336 schools [6] (Fig. 5) show that home-room advisers give more attention to non-guidance administrative duties than to guidance. It is, of course, possible that guidance may be rendered through the performance of administrative duties, such as discipline,

DUTIES PERFORMED BY HOME-ROOM ADVISERS	PER CENT	
1. Discipline	69.0	
2. Oversight of social conduct	65.5	
3. Direction of special home-room activities	74.8	
4. Guidance concerning quality of work	61.9	
5. Curriculum guidance	61.3	
6. Vocational guidance	29.2	

FIGURE 5.—Percentages of duties specified which were performed by home-room advisers in 336 secondary schools

oversight of social conduct, and direction of special home-room activities. However, since the duties are general rather than specific, the guidance values are likely to be only incidental. Nearly two-thirds of the home-room advisers give guidance concerning the choice of curriculums and the quality of classroom work. Only about a third of the advisers give vocational guidance. The findings do not indicate the breadth of guidance service to be desired, although the guidance activities carried on compare favorably with

6 Koos, Leonard V., and Kefauver, Grayson N., op. cit., p 546.

those of administrative officers in schools in which the home-room organization is not employed.

Certain schools have introduced class directors, class guides, class supervisors, and class principals to organize and direct the work of the home-room advisers and to unify the guidance activities for the different class groups. These directors supply a type of special service to the home-room work which widens the scope and gives balance to the guidance activities.

Teachers as advisers.—The data presented in Figure 2 showed that teachers were utilized as advisers in approximately a fifth of the schools with enrollments of fewer than 200 and a thirteenth of the schools with enrollments of more than 1,000. The practice of utilizing teachers in large proportions as guidance functionaries is followed chiefly by the smaller schools and signifies usually the absence of a guidance organization, although many of the duties carried on by administrative officers and home-room advisers are assumed by the teachers in the capacity of guidance functionaries. With proper training for the performance of guidance activities, teachers may in the course of time become skilled home-room advisers or special counselors, but as a rule their guidance activities are more or less general.

Trained counselors as guidance functionaries.—Whether the emphasis is placed on the vocational, educational, or personal aspects of guidance, certain schools have conceived of the activities of counseling and guidance as involving knowledge and technical skill beyond that possessed by the teacher and general administrative officer. Such schools regard guidance as an act of skill, which requires for its successful execution training of a technical character. Accordingly, in these schools guidance becomes the responsibility of the specialist, who may be developed from the staff through special training or be added to the staff for the specific purpose.

To develop a satisfactory program of guidance through special counselors requires that the counselors become members of the school's staff and that the duties to be performed be defined and relations to staff members clearly established. The use of the specialist in guidance does not render unnecessary the assumption of certain general guidance responsibilities by teachers and administrative officers. It merely requires a differentiation of duties with the specialist and the generalist accepting responsibility for the activities each can most successfully perform. If the time of the specialist is used in the performance of duties that properly belong to the generalist or the generalist undertakes to perform the duties requiring special training and skill, the guidance program will fail because of faulty organization.

The development of the guidance program around the counselor in the local school makes possible a type of guidance often slighted in schools which depend chiefly on the administrative officers plus the services of outside specialists available only on call. However, the success of the plan will depend on the limitations imposed. If the counselor is overloaded with pupils or is expected to divert energy to other administrative work, the results accomplished may vary only slightly from those obtained through other plans.

Objective data [7] for schools which emphasize the teacher-adviser and the special-counselor plans show that the advisers perform administrative duties related to guidance, such as discipline, oversight of social conduct, and counseling concerning the quality of work to a greater extent than the counselors. (Fig. 6.) On the contrary, the counselors surpass the advisers in the frequency of performance of the more specialized types of guidance, such as curriculum guidance, vocational guidance, placement advisement, and follow-up service. While the differences in the distribution of time of the different types of duties indicated are not large, they are, nevertheless, significant. As a result it can be concluded that the adoption of the special-counselor plan increases the performance of the specialized guidance activities by counselors and decreases those that are partly administrative in character.

Guidance committees.—In about a fifth (20.4 per cent) of the schools with enrollments of more than 1,000, committees of teachers carry on the guidance work. These functionaries are usually released from some teaching duties or are paid a fixed amount for the responsibilities assumed. The plan enables a principal to select from his staff teachers best qualified for guidance work, to establish standards of training

---

[7] Koos, Leonard V., *and* Kefauver, Grayson N., op. cit., pp. 562-564.

for the advisory committee, and to effect a continuing organization for the guidance service. The committee organization represents a stage between the home-room or teacher-adviser organization and the special-counselor plan. The members of guidance committees as a rule are not specialists in guidance work, although they may be looked upon as potential specialists.

The guidance committee is seldom found in the small schools with enrollments of fewer than 200, the percentage of frequency in the sampling of 336 schools [8] being only 2.7.

The visiting teacher.—The visiting teacher is utilized as a guidance functionary in the large schools with enrollments in

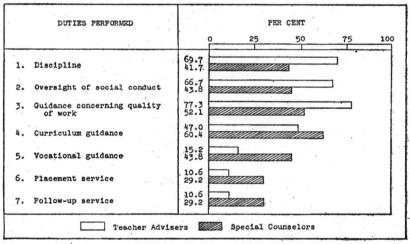

FIGURE 6.—Percentages of teacher advisers and special counselors carrying on the guidance activities specified in 336 secondary schools

excess of 1,000 to about the same extent as the guidance committee. She is often a trained social worker, and in some instances a psychiatric social worker. The training is seldom the same as that of a special counselor, although the work of the visiting teacher is indispensable in pupil counseling. In some schools the visiting teacher has superseded the attendance officer, and as a result is responsible for both attendance and home adjustments, both of which are essential to guidance work. Only a small percentage (5.4) of the 336 schools studied by Koos and Kefauver [9] were found to possess this functionary, a fact accounted for chiefly by the special character of the visiting teacher's work.

---

[8] Koos Leonard V., *and* Kefauver, Grayson N., op. cit., p. 516.
[9] Ibid., p. 516.

CHAPTER III : GUIDANCE ACTIVITIES IN SECONDARY SCHOOLS

The types of guidance activities carried on.—The guidance activities carried on in secondary schools are numerous and varied. Analysis of the activities of guidance functionaries made by French [1] as a part of the Commonwealth Study of Teacher Training resulted in a master list of 180 specific activities which were considered to relate to guidance in secondary schools. An evaluation of these activities by counselors and by experts in education provides classified lists arranged in order of frequency of performance and in order of importance. The correlations between frequency of performance of activities and their relative importance as determined by counselors reveal certain strengths and weaknesses in the guidance activities carried on by the principal and his assistants in the secondary schools. In activities which involved advising with parents, counseling with individual pupils, and advising with pupils in groups the correlations are high, being 0.767, 0.742, and 0.728, respectively; in activities pertaining to cooperation with community agencies and with teachers the correlations are medium (0.404 and 0.316); in activities involving the collecting and recording of data and assisting in extracurriculum activities the correlations are low (0.265 and 0.113).

In the school systems and individual schools visited by the members of the survey staff a great variety of activities in guidance were being carried on. Certain of the more frequent and significant ones will be described in the following paragraphs.

(1) *Instructing pupils regarding occupations.*—The most common method of informing pupils regarding occupations is the course in occupations. Some incidental information

---

[1] French, Fannie. An Analysis of Activities Involved in Pupil Guidance, pp. 30-41. Unpublished master's thesis, Department of Education, University of Chicago, 1926.

regarding occupations is no doubt secured by pupils from the teachers of the various school subjects. Such information is unorganized and frequently inaccurate. These conditions make systematic instruction in occupations necessary if the pupil is to secure a knowledge of opportunities in occupations and to develop some degree of understanding of the work of the world.

Not all schools provide courses in occupations. A recent sampling study [2] of 208 secondary schools in New Jersey showed that only 60, or 31.9 per cent, offered courses in occupations. Data presented by Koos and Kefauver [3] show that the courses in occupations are offered in all grades of the secondary school (7–12), although the dominance of practice favors the ninth grade.

The occupations selected for study in some of the courses are local in character, while in others the occupations are general. In some schools a general textbook on occupations is used; a number of such textbooks are now available for general courses in occupations. The prevailing practice is to offer the courses five hours per week for one semester or three hours per week for two semesters.[4] In some of the schools the pupil is required to prepare a career book of some occupation in which he is interested. The purpose of the career book is to induce intensive study of an occupation in contrast with the extensive study of the occupations considered in the occupation course.

The practice of providing instruction in occupations is in harmony with the purposes of guidance from its beginning. The failure of the practice to obtain a stronger place among the guidance activities of the schools is probably due to the inability of regular teachers and administrative officers to meet the responsibility successfully—a fact which, if true, argues strongly for the standard adopted by the National Vocational Guidance Association, namely, that vocational guidance should be offered only by qualified persons.

(2) *Carrying on occupational research.*—Interest in occupations is enhanced by current information regarding occu-

---

[2] Cunliffe, Rex B. Guidance Practice in New Jersey, p. 6. Studies in Education, No. 2. Rutgers University, School of Education, New Brunswick, N. J.

[3] Guidance in Secondary Schools, p. 93. New York, Macmillan Co., 1932.

[4] Ibid., p. 96.

pations and by reliable recent information regarding local occupations and their demands for workers. Such information is rarely obtainable in organized form. It must be collected, organized, and interpreted. This is the task of the instructor of courses in occupations or the department of guidance. The activity is fundamental to vocational guidance in a school or system of schools.

Occupational research is a more conspicuous feature of the guidance work in the large city school systems than in the individual schools studied in this investigation. Perhaps it is more necessary in the large city systems than in the individual schools in the smaller communities. In the latter, occupational information is secured to a greater extent by incidental means than in the larger communities. However, information secured incidentally can not be an adequate substitute for information secured systematically as a result of occupational research.

Examples of occupational research are given in the case studies of Chicago, Cincinnati, and Providence reported in Chapters IV, V, and VI. The occupational information made available through research in these systems contributes very materially to occupational guidance in their individual schools.

(3) *Rendering placement service.*—In the large school systems placement service is rendered through the bureau of guidance, a division of the bureau of guidance, the counselors in the local schools, or the instructors in vocational schools. In the individual secondary schools in the smaller cities the service is rendered through the director of guidance or the administrative officers. Placement service is desired by pupils who leave school before graduation or who enter upon a life pursuit immediately after graduation.

The services which can be rendered by the school in occupational placement are finding positions for pupils, directing the pupils in their search for employment, answering requests of employers for information regarding pupils applying for employment, and assisting pupils in making adjustments after securing employment. These services require extensive knowledge of both pupils and employment conditions.

On account of the technical character of placement services many schools neglect the responsibility. The sampling data collected by Cunliffe [5] in New Jersey show that only 14.9 per cent of the secondary schools investigated assume responsibility for placement. These findings are quite at variance with an earlier study by Edgerton and Herr for 256 senior high schools, 379 junior high schools, and 178 part-time schools,[6] in which it was found that 69 per cent of the schools offered vocational placement service for part-time and full-time employment. The difference may in part be accounted for by the fact that the latter sampling consisted chiefly of large schools, while the former consisted largely of small schools in villages, towns, and small cities.

(4) *Making follow-up investigations.*—Two of the school systems studied in this project carry on systematic follow-up investigations of graduates at intervals up to five years. The other systems and individual schools neglect this type of investigation, restricting their efforts to the follow-up of pupils who have withdrawn from school to enter upon employment. Both types of follow-up investigations are important. The latter possesses the greater value to the individual pupil concerned, but the former is essential in planning programs of studies, in the reorganization of curriculums, and in projecting programs of guidance.

The follow-up investigation may be carried on as a project of the central bureau after the method of occupational research discussed in section 2 of this chapter, or as a project of the class counselor as described by Allen.[7] The latter method is superior in that it is carried on by the person who is both immediately and personally interested in the findings of such investigations.

(5) *Effecting adjustments between employees and employer.*— A guidance service to part-time workers, and in some instances to pupils who have withdrawn from school to enter full-time employment, is rendered by counselors and placement officers in effecting adjustments between the young employees and their employers. In businesses and industries which maintain

[5] Cunliffe, Rex B., op. cit., p. 6.

[6] Edgerton, A. H., *and* Herr, L. A. Present Status of Guidance Activities in Secondary Schools. The Twenty-third Yearbook, Part II, p. 39. National Society for the Study of Education, 1924.

[7] Allen, Richard D. The Continuous Follow-up Survey in the Senior High School. Junior-Senior High School Clearing House, 7: 44–49, September, 1932.

personnel directors the adjustment of the workers is often regarded as a mutual responsibility of employer and school. In institutions which do not maintain personnel directors the adjustment of the young worker presents a difficult problem, which places great responsibility on the guidance department of the school, if the welfare of the former pupil is regarded as a matter of school concern.

The study by Edgerton and Herr[8] showed that approximately a third (34.3 per cent) of the counselors in 115 senior high schools, 154 junior high schools, and 66 part-time schools cooperated with employers' associations, personnel managers, labor organizations, etc., in promoting the welfare of young people transferring to business or industry from school. The data indicate that school functionaries are not strongly inclined to carry their guidance activities beyond the portals of the school.

(6) *Visiting homes of pupils.*—In the schools with counselors or visiting teachers the homes of pupils are visited when it is considered necessary to secure the cooperation of parents and to gather case data regarding the family history and environmental background of pupils. These visits usually yield better results when made by trained counselors, visiting teachers, and psychiatric social workers than when made by home-room teachers and administrative officers. The service is important in guidance work and frequently results in the better adjustment of pupils to school and in a wiser choice of occupation.

Data are not available to show the extent of home visitation by the different guidance functionaries. In the case of home-room advisers in the schools studied by Koos and Kefauver,[9] it is disclosed that home visitation is a little more frequent in junior high schools than in the senior and 4-year high schools, and that the homes of problem cases and failing pupils are visited more frequently than the homes of other pupils. The practice of visiting the homes of all pupils by the home-room advisers was followed in 13.3 per cent of the junior high schools and 7.2 per cent of the senior and 4-year high schools.

---

8 Edgerton, A. H., *and* Herr, L. A., op. cit., p. 54.

9 Koos, Leonard V., *and* Kefauver, Grayson N., op. cit., p. 549.

(7) *Compiling case histories of pupils.*—On account of the labor involved in the collection, analysis, interpretation, and writing of case reports, the case history is usually compiled only for problem pupils. It is not possible to compile case histories of pupils generally in the majority of secondary schools since complete data are not assembled for all pupils. Only 38.1 per cent of the 522 schools studied by Reavis and Woellner[10] reported the use of cumulative folders for the filing of case data regarding pupils. Most schools (89.7 per cent), however, were found to keep cumulative records of the progress of individual pupils, thus making possible the compilation of case histories when supplemented by information collected through guidance activities.

Case histories of problem pupils were available in the files of most of the school systems and individual schools visited by the members of the survey staff investigating guidance programs. Evidently the practice is encouraged in the schools which have well-developed programs of guidance. The use of the method presupposes the keeping of adequate records, the careful study of cumulative data, and the pursuit of the cases until their culmination.

(8) *Administering tests to pupils.*—Data secured from tests of mental ability, achievement in the school subjects, and nonintellectual qualities are considered essential in guidance. Some of these tests may be given by administrative officers and teachers in connection with admission, classification, and diagnostic and remedial instruction. Others must be administered by the guidance functionaries of the schools to pupils as individuals or in groups for the purpose of securing data needed in counseling.

Approximately half (52.1 per cent) of the secondary schools studied in New Jersey by Cunliffe[11] considered the test program as a guidance activity. Whether the tests are administered by guidance functionaries, teachers, or administrative officers is not specified, but the implication is clear, namely, that the activities involved in the collection of test data belong in the field of guidance. That some of the tests employed in guidance are administered by guidance functionaries can not be doubted in the light of the information

[10] Cunliffe, Rex B., op. cit., p. 129.
[11] Op. cit., p. 6.

[21]

supplied by Koos and Kefauver[12] regarding types of tests used in guidance and the frequency of their use.

In school systems with bureaus of guidance the administration of tests for purposes of guidance is regarded as a specialized function to be carried on by a department of the bureau. In individual schools the activity is usually performed by the counselor. In either case the purpose of the activity is the collection of information for use in counseling and guidance.

(9) *Preparing guidance bulletins.*—Bulletins of information, such as pamphlets on occupations, news notes of current developments in occupations, bulletins on programs of studies, circulars on college entrance, school handbooks, guidance issues of the school paper, and selected lists of books on occupations, are prepared in many secondary schools for the guidance of pupils. While some or all of these publications may be prepared by committees of teachers and pupils, much of the information must be supplied by guidance functionaries. The collection of information suitable for publication and the editorial preparation of the information are considered important guidance activities in certain schools.

In large cities having guidance bureaus a considerable portion of the guidance functionaries' time may be consumed and no small portion of the guidance budget used in this activity. Examples of such utilization of time and money will be found in the case studies of Chicago and Cincinnati.

(10) *Giving information to pupils in groups.*—Guidance functionaries in the schools studied in this investigation observe the practice of giving information to pupils at the time of admission to the secondary school regarding the selection of a secondary school in the large school systems and regarding the choice of curriculums or subjects in the school to which admission is sought. A guidance functionary frequently visits the elementary schools from which the pupils come and provides the pupils with the information needed or meets the pupils in groups at the receiving secondary school. The service is intended as an aid to pupils and parents in making a selection of the opportunities offered by secondary schools. Evidence is presented in at least one of the schools studied to show the value of the service to pupils.

---

12 Koos, Leonard V., *and* Kefauver, Grayson N., op. cit., p. 282.

Information is also given to pupils in groups early in the high-school course regarding colleges and entrance requirements in order that the pupils looking forward to college may be duly informed of admission conditions. Some schools provide individual conferences with pupils or parents on request, but in general the individual conference is not considered necessary.

The plan of giving information to pupils in groups makes for economy in guidance, provided that the information is correct and is effectively presented.

(11) *Counseling individual pupils.*—Advising with individual pupils in need of counsel is an important activity in any guidance program. The interview may be sought voluntarily by the pupil or at the request of parent, teacher, or administrative officer. In some schools interviews with individual pupils are scheduled by counselors as a means of providing every pupil with the opportunity to secure individual guidance.

Individual counseling to be successful requires technical knowledge and skill scarcely to be expected in some of the functionaries who undertake to render guidance services in secondary schools. As a result some of the individual counseling is little more than perfunctory interviewing. A background of personal knowledge of the pupil is required by the counselor as a basis for the interview. This involves cumulative records, the results of tests, personality ratings, and current reports of school progress. Even with adequate information the counselor may defeat the purpose of the individual interview unless the technique of interviewing is thoroughly understood and skillfully practiced. Adequate follow-up must then be planned to check the results of the interview and to provide further counsel when considered necessary.

In an extensive survey involving 8,594 secondary schools, Billett [13] finds that 28 distinct methods are employed for meeting the individual differences of pupils, such as variation in the number of subjects a pupil is permitted to carry, special coaching of slow pupils, special classes for pupils who have failed, adjustment classes or rooms, remedial classes or rooms,

[13] Billett, Roy O. What the High Schools are Doing for the Individual. School Life, 16: 87, January, 1931.

differentiated assignments to pupils in the same class or section, and the like. The effective use of any of these plans of providing for individual differences in pupils presupposes individual counseling both in making the diagnosis of individual differences and in enlisting the cooperation of the pupil in improving the ability of the individual or in compensating for the disability found to exist.

In the schools and school systems described in later chapters of the present report, individual counseling is found to occupy a prominent place in the guidance programs. Marked differences are found, however, both in the character of individual counseling practiced and in the emphasis given to this phase of school guidance.

(12) *Holding case conferences with groups.*—The sheer magnitude of the guidance problem in large school systems and in large secondary schools requires that guidance functionaries deal with pupils in groups. The method is not considered an adequate substitute for individual counseling, yet it offers promise of good results if correct techniques are employed. At times the entire pupil body of the school may be instructed and advised in the school assembly, or class groups in class meetings. School or class opinion may thus be directed and attitudes and ideals formed.

A method considered effective for class groups is the case conference. Case material is placed before the group and the conference is carried on under the direction of the guidance functionary somewhat similar to case instruction in schools of law. With proper material and desirable conference technique superior results may be obtained. However, with poor material and poor technique such counseling may prove worse than none because of the potential dangers of developing undesirable attitudes and ideals on the part of the pupils.

The method is used only to a limited extent in the schools studied by the investigators, but it appears to merit experimental study and wider application than is now received.

(13) *Sponsoring pupil activities.*—Guidance functionaries as a rule should not be used as regular sponsors of pupil activities. However, certain activities may offer such large opportunities for guidance that the assignment of a guidance

functionary to sponsorship of an activity is highly desirable. Examples of such sponsorship are found in leadership clubs, pupil-government organizations, and alumni organizations.

(14) *Conferring with teachers and sponsors regarding individual pupils.*—The relation of guidance functionaries to teachers and sponsors is usually consultative rather than supervisory or executive. Hence, conferences between guidance functionaries and teachers or sponsors should be regarded in a spirit of mutuality of interest and concern for the welfare of the pupil about whom the conference is held. The conference may be initiated by guidance functionary or by teacher or sponsor. In either case the purpose is virtually the same, namely, to furnish or to receive information and under certain conditions advice regarding an individual pupil.

Lack of articulation and coordination between guidance functionaries on the one hand and teachers and sponsors on the other have hindered the guidance service in many schools. The articulation desired is furthered by proper administrative organization and by the cultivation on the part of the entire staff of a vital interest in the welfare of the individual pupil. The definition of the relations of guidance functionaries to teachers and sponsors should do much to promote articulation and to coordinate the activities of counseling with the general program of education.

(15) *Serving on committees of teachers to develop material for try-out courses.*—The guidance value of try-out courses is enhanced if the materials of the course are produced by committee action of the teachers involved and the guidance functionaries. A sense of personal responsibility for the course on the part of the teacher is combined with the technical contribution of the guidance functionaries. Furthermore, through cooperative effort, mutual understanding of the purposes of guidance and the use of try-out materials as a means to the desired end is secured.

Satisfactory service on committees for the development of try-out courses may lead to similar service in the development of orientation courses and to courses in subject-matter departments. Examples were found in some of the schools studied of such usefulness on the part of guidance functionaries.

(16) *Conducting guidance clinics.*—Guidance clinics for the diagnosis of certain types of problem cases were promoted by the guidance functionaries in some of the schools represented in this project. The guidance functionary may participate in the work of the clinic or act as executive secretary in securing the services of specialists and in the preparation of case reports. The purpose of the clinics is to secure for an individual pupil a type of service without which the efforts of the school and the pupil fail to secure satisfactory results. The guidance clinic appears to be as necessary as a clinic for orthopedic defects, speech disabilities, or other organic conditions. It may be the means of correcting behavior difficulties in pupils or in solving learning problems.

(17) *Making reports of activities to administrative officers.*— Reports of activities by guidance functionaries to administrative officers constitute a valuable test of worth of the guidance services. Critical reactions of administrative officers to the activities engaged in by the guidance functionaries, self-criticism resulting from analysis of activities in the preparation of reports, justification of activities in terms of budget costs, and the use of guidance data in the development of school policies and curriculum and extracurriculum work should result in the improvement of guidance activities.

Mechanical recounting of activities, such as number of parents interviewed, number of bulletins distributed, and number of pupils advised, is of little consequence. Case reports, bulletins prepared, follow-up data secured, failing pupils salvaged, and the like afford evidence of guidance activities which concern administrative officers and teachers as well as the guidance functionaries.

(18) *Miscellaneous activities.*—Other activities closely related to those described in the foregoing paragraphs were also observed in the school systems and schools visited by the investigators of the survey staff. However, the 17 types of activities discussed are believed to be sufficiently representative of the more important duties of guidance functionaries to render the discussion of other activities unnecessary, especially since numerous aspects of counseling and guidance are considered in the case reports of guidance programs in most of the remaining chapters of this monograph.

CHAPTER IV : CASE REPORT ON BOSTON

The beginning of guidance in Boston.—The schools of Boston are thought to be the first in the United States to provide organized vocational guidance for pupils. In 1910 the school committee accepted the plan of a special committee, composed of masters and a representative of the Vocation Bureau established two years previously at the Civic Service House in Boston, that a teacher be designated in each elementary and secondary school of the city to act as vocational counselor. Vocational guidance thus became a regular feature of the school system in Boston and has continued to the present time.

The organization of a department of vocational guidance.— The Department of Vocational Guidance was organized in 1915 with an acting director of vocational guidance in charge. During the previous year this officer gave half time as director of vocational counselors and head of the division of assignments and records at the Continuation School, and the other half was in charge of the Boston Placement Bureau, with which she had been associated since its establishment in 1912.

In 1916 the appointment of this same officer as director was confirmed and responsibility for guidance and placement and follow-up, as well as direction of the school counselors, was placed in the new department. The organization developed for the department is shown in Figure 7.

At the present time the personnel of the department consists of the director, 6 vocational instructors (men), 11 vocational assistants (women), and 2 clerks. This staff of workers is responsible for guidance, placement, and follow-up service in the city schools. Nearly all the vocational instructors and assistants are assigned to part-time service in the high schools (four give full time). One gives part time in three intermediate schools. The others spend the remainder of their time in carrying on guidance, placement, and follow-up duties at the departmental office.

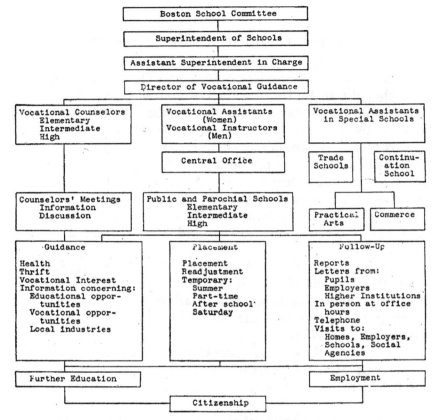

FIGURE 7.—Organization and functions of the Vocational Guidance Department, Boston, Mass.

The objectives of the department.—The objectives of the Department of Vocational Guidance as stated by the director are the following:

I. Educational and vocational guidance:
   1. To assist pupils to a knowledge of educational and vocational possibilities.
   2. To assist pupils to a knowledge of the common occupations and an understanding of the problems of the occupational world so that they may prepare more fully for lives of usefulness in the community. Vocational and political citizenship must go hand in hand.

3. To obtain for each pupil, as far as possible, **every** opportunity which it is the duty of the public schools to provide.

4. To aid pupils to realize their educational or vocational aims.

II. Placement:

1. To assist graduates and undergraduates, who must leave school to work, in finding suitable positions. Physical and mental fitness, school preparation, and vocational interests are the determining factors in placement.

2. To aid those who need readjustment in their work.

3. To aid those who, in order to continue their school work, must have after-school work, Saturday or summer work.

III. Follow-up:

1. To help young workers to a better understanding of their relationships to other workers in their own and other occupations and to society.

2. To insure better cooperation between the public schools on one hand and the higher educational institutions on the various commercial and industrial pursuits on the other hand, in order that there may be no gap between the groups.

3. To make scientific studies of the information gathered for the benefit of the child, the school, the employer, and society.

4. To assist in adapting the schools to the needs of the pupils and the community, through providing the information needed for the modification of curriculum materials.

Duties of the director.—The director is the chief officer of the Department of Vocational Guidance responsible to the superintendent of schools through an assistant superintendent. The director is responsible for the policies of the department, making the budget, and directing the general supervision of the department staff. In the individual schools the director is a staff officer, acting as a consultant to the principal in carrying on the guidance activities desired through the school counselor. Executive authority is not exercised in individual schools by the director.

Continuity has been given to the policies and activities of the Department of Vocational Guidance by the fact that the present director, Miss Susan J. Ginn, has served as head of the department from its establishment in 1915.

[29]

Duties of instructors and assistants.—The duties of the vocational instructors and assistants are functional in character and are assigned by the director of the department. At the request of a principal, an instructor or assistant may be assigned to part-time or full-time duties in a given school. The duties usually consist of personal interviews at the request of pupils or principal, registration and personal interviews of the entire freshman and senior classes and of junior and sophomore classes when time permits, instruction in occupations, placement, and follow-up investigations. The program of the instructors and assistants is not rigidly standardized, but is subject to modification in the light of the needs of a school.

The office duties of the instructors and assistants are partly departmental and partly functional. For example, each instructor and assistant may be responsible for the guidance, placement, and follow-up work in a given group of schools. In addition, certain functional assignments may be given to each, such as maintenance of evening office hours twice per month, conduct of a particular follow-up investigation, preparation of reports, and the like.

Duties of school counselors.—The counselors are representatives of the Department of Vocational Guidance in the individual schools. They are teachers, submasters, or masters' assistants and usually carry a full teaching load, although they may be released from teaching duties for counseling by by the principals.

The duties of the counselors are:

1. To be the representative of the Department of Vocational Guidance in the district.
2. To attend all meetings of counselors called by the Director of Vocational Guidance.
3. To be responsible for all material sent out to the school by the Department of Vocational Guidance.
4. To gather and keep on file occupational information.
5. To arrange with the local branch librarians about shelves of books bearing upon educational and vocational guidance.
6. To recommend that teachers show the relationship of their work to occupational problems.
7. To interview pupils in grades 6 and above who are failing, attempt to find the reason, and suggest remedy.
8. To make use of the cumulative record card when advising children.

9. To consult records of intelligence tests when advising children.

10. To make a careful study with grades 7 and 8 of the bulletin Guide to the Choice of a Secondary School.

11. To urge children to remain in school.

12. To recommend conferences with parents of children who are failing or leaving school.

13. To interview and check cards of all children leaving school, making clear to them the requirements for obtaining working certificates.

14. To be responsible for filling in the applications of pupils for employment certificates and communicating, with recommendations, to the Department of Vocational Guidance.

The quality of service rendered by a counselor in a given school will naturally vary with the factors which condition it, such as the attitude of the principal toward guidance, the training of the teachers for guidance responsibility, and the time of the individual counselor available for guidance duties. However, the presence of representatives of the Department of Vocational Guidance in all high schools of the city and a few of the intermediate schools makes for unification of the guidance work and acts as a centripetal force for a centralized organization.

Interschool and curriculum guidance.—The selection of schools and the choice of curriculum offerings by a pupil in a system of the size and complicated organization of Boston is no easy task. Choices of intermediate schools in many districts must be made at the end of the sixth grade. Since the intermediate schools have multiple curriculums and prevocational training, occupational guidance is needed by the pupil prior to admission and during his residence in the intermediate school. Selection of a senior high school at the end of the ninth grade or regular high school at the end of the eighth grade requires vocational choice on the part of the pupil, inasmuch as the offerings of the different schools are somewhat specialized in character.

As an aid to the pupils in choosing a secondary school, a bulletin has been prepared by the Department of Vocational Guidance. This bulletin is distributed through the school counselors to pupils and parents, and conferences are held with the pupils both in groups and individually by the counselors during supervised study periods. Effort is put forth by the counselors to aid the pupils in making an intelligent choice of a secondary school and courses within the school. The choice requires a consideration of occupations.

In the general high schools the work of counselor is taken over partly or wholly by the vocational instructors or assistants. After admission the pupil is advised regarding his school progress, part-time work in vacation periods, selection of extracurriculum activities, and is counseled regarding placement, if withdrawal from school is found necessary. In the special high schools in which choice of vocation has been made prior to admission, the counselor or vocational instructor or assistant is expected to be reponsible for the adjustment of the pupil to his school work, assistance to the pupil in self-analysis of abilities and the selection of phases of the occupation chosen in which the abilities possessed offer greatest promise of success, the choice of higher schools, assistance in the placement of the pupil for part-time or full-time employment, and the follow-up of the pupil in case of withdrawal and after graduation.

Successful guidance of the types described requires training and release from teaching responsibility on the part of counselors. The Department of Vocational Guidance undertakes to supply general training for counseling, but the work in some of the intermediate schools and special high schools requires technical training and ability frequently not possessed by the school counselors. In such instances the director of the department, at the request of the principal, has assigned a staff member to the school in question for part-time service and in some cases full-time service.

Counseling and guidance.—From the beginning in Boston the emphasis of the Department of Vocational Guidance has been placed on educational and occupational counseling and guidance. This does not mean that the other aspects of guidance, often referred to as ethical, social, personal, physical guidance, etc., are neglected or altogether overlooked. The concept, vocational guidance, is used by the department in a broad sense. It includes all services in counseling which may ultimately lead an individual to a successful choice of an occupation. For example, the intelligent choice of a secondary school requires occupational information and tentative choice of vocation. The counseling of an individual

with respect to his choice of school involves careful consideration of his educational progress, abilities, disabilities, interests,
and economic conditions. These aspects of guidance thus
become means to the end of occupational guidance.

The services within the school commonly designated as
pupil adjustment are responsibilities of teachers and principal as well as of the guidance department, although in
schools enjoying the services of vocational instructors or
assistants of the department, aid in effecting educational
adjustments is usually rendered. Broadly speaking, the
work of the department is to give educational and occupational information and to counsel pupils with respect to
adjustments in school as well as to vocations.

In the seventh, eighth, and ninth grades one hour each
week has been set aside in the schedule for group instruction
in educational and vocational guidance. A tentative plan
for the use of the time has been prepared by a committee of
five representing the intermediate schools and the Department of Vocational Guidance. The plan consists of flexible
units designed to aid pupils in discovering their interests and
aptitudes and to give information that will aid them in
choosing wisely not only for the present but for their future
work.

Placement service.—Placement service in Boston has been a
responsibility of the Department of Vocational Guidance
from the time the services of the Placement Bureau were
available. This bureau was completely absorbed by the
department in 1917. The importance of the service is
indicated by data furnished by the department showing
that approximately 60 per cent of the recent graduates of 10
high schools were either working or seeking work within a
year after graduation. About half of these graduates sought
the assistance of the department in finding employment and
about half secured placement through the department's aid.

Despite the fact that the department strives to keep children in school until graduation from high school and to encourage further training on the part of promising high-school
graduates, the demand for part-time placement service prior
to graduation is heavy. Requests for assistance in securing
vacation employment, part-time employment, and employ-

ment by pupils unable to continue to graduation because of economic conditions and lack of sufficient ability are numerous. The department, through its central office and its instructors, assistants, and counselors in individual schools, undertakes not only to find positions for these pupils but also to secure employment in which the individuals are interested and are likely to prove successful.

Placement service is refused when the records show that an individual is physically unfit or otherwise unequal to the work or when arrangements can be made to keep the pupil in school. The counselors in the schools are of great assistance to the department in rendering advice regarding placement applications.

The work of the department is so organized that all the members have responsibility for placement service. This requires all members to keep in close touch with placement opportunities and the types of individuals for whom opportunities are available. Furthermore, complete knowledge of the applicants for placement is required before placement is attempted. The purpose of the department is to render mutual service to employer and employed. Such service can not be rendered by novices. It requires training and adequate information based on comprehensive records and research.

Follow-up work.—The State requires that every pupil who has been in a trade school for six months or more shall be followed for a period of five years. The follow-up of all graduates of the general high schools and the Girls' Latin and Mechanic Arts High School is carried on in various ways, namely: (1) Letters from the Department of Vocational Guidance; (2) visits to employers by instructors, assistants, and school instructors; (3) visits to the homes, telephone calls; and (4) visits by the pupils at the evening office hours of the department. Voluntary follow-up studies are carried on by the department as research investigations for purposes of obtaining guidance material and information which may affect the curriculums of the schools.

The primary purpose of the follow-up investigation as an aspect of guidance is service to the individual who has withdrawn from or completed the work of the school. Through follow-up contacts the department is able to continue a public service on the part of the school which may result in the adjustment of the former pupil to employment or further education. The information thus secured, if used, makes possible the scientific evaluation of programs of study, the revision of curriculums, and the guidance of pupils with respect to occupational requirements and opportunities.

Since 1916 the Department of Vocational Guidance has followed up the graduates of all the general high schools (Dorchester High School since 1924) and the Mechanic Arts High School and Boston Trade School within one year after graduation. The Girls' Latin School was recently added to the list. Five-year follow-up studies have been made since 1926 for the English High School, Brighton High School, Charleston High School, East Boston High School, Hyde Park High School, South Boston High School, Jamaica Plain High School, Mechanic Arts High School, and Girls' High School. A copy of the report, which includes a general summary and the story of each member of the graduating class, is sent to each headmaster and vocational counselor in order that they may see what has happened to the product of their school.

Guidance in the Mechanic Arts High School.—The problem of providing vocational guidance has been met in the Mechanic Arts High School for boys by the assignment of one of the vocational instructors of the department staff to the school on a full-time basis (four-fifths in the school itself, one-fifth at the central office in the interest of that school's graduates). This school offers technical training for boys preparing to enter some occupation requiring mechanical experience. It does not train for particular trades, but undertakes to provide shopwork and drawing that will facilitate adjustment in mechanical pursuits. Two curriculums are offered, namely, the shop or mechanical curriculum and the technical preparatory curriculum. In the curriculum first mentioned the boy may specialize in some kind of shopwork after the first year or in electrical laboratory work, machine design, architectural drawing, or industrial design. In the second curriculum less time is devoted to shopwork and drawing and more to the subjects required for admission to technical schools.

[35]

The vocational instructor in this school advises with pupils individually regarding the choice of a vocation or higher technical school; prepares guidance material for the use of regular teachers in the social studies to be taught 30 class periods in the ninth grade and supervises the teaching; plans meetings of the alumni association of the school twice each year as a means of making contacts with the graduates; encourages the keeping of guidance bulletin boards in all of the home rooms for the purpose of, incidental guidance; and gives systematic instruction two periods a week to seniors in class groups in vocational guidance, requiring the keeping of a notebook by each pupil and the preparation of four lengthy reports in cooperation with the English department. The instructor keeps a cumulative record card of each pupil; visits the home of a pupil when necessary to secure parental cooperation or advice; keeps office hours at the noon recess in order that the boys may come on their own time for conference; visits industries to interest employers in the graduates, to see how those employed are getting along, and to provide for future placements; and makes follow-up studies of all graduates for a period of five years.

Vocational guidance is made an integral part of the work of the Mechanic Arts High School. Since the work is in the hands of a trained instructor who is a member of the staff of the Department of Vocational Guidance, the school has an advantage not possessed by all the schools of the city.

Two regular teachers are allowed five periods each week to do the individual counseling in the second and third years. Both of these teachers have taken courses in vocational guidance. These teachers are under the supervision of the vocational instructor assigned from the Department of Vocational Guidance.

Guidance in the Michelángelo Intermediate School.—The guidance work in the Michelangelo Intermediate School presents a problem of greater difficulty than that in the average intermediate school. The pupils are largely foreign, chiefly of Italian parentage. Language difficulties make for retardation and economic conditions for early employment. Educational guidance, personal interviews, classes in occupational information, follow-up work in the ninth grade, part-time employment, and placement service constitute the major aspects of the work of the vocational assistant assigned by the department to this school.

Through the interest of one of the leading industries and with the approval of the school committee, the vocational assistant has carried on an interesting experiment in cooperative work and schooling with girls. In June, 1926, 30 girls were induced to give up poor jobs in which they were unhappy and to try the new plan, which consisted in dividing the group into two divisions and rotating them by weeks in school and at work. Improved working conditions, better pay, better morale, and opportunity to continue schooling made the plan successful both to the girls and the employer. In the course of time the experiment grew to include approximately 200 girls. The majority of the girls were enrolled in the intermediate grades and housed in the Continuation School. Some were in the tenth grade of the High School of Practical Arts. Several were subsequently graduated from this latter school, one with honors.

Recent changes in the management of the industry have resulted in some modification in the plan. However, from the point of view of the cooperating schools, the Department of Vocational Guidance, and the girls concerned, the original experiment was regarded as significant and worthy of repetition, particularly for pupils of continuation-school age in need of employment.

Cost of vocational guidance.—By act of the General Assembly of Massachusetts in 1925 the School Committee of Boston is permitted to levy $0.03 on each $1,000 of the valuation of the city of Boston for vocational guidance purposes. This authorization made possible in 1931 a budget of approximately $60,000. The enrollment of all the high schools was about 26,000, of the ninth grade in intermediate schools about 4,000, and of the seventh and eighth grades about 20,000—total enrollment for the secondary-school grades of approximately 50,000. If the guidance activities of the department were restricted to pupils of secondary-school grades, the resources available would be about $1.20 per pupil. If the enrollment of the sixth grade is added, which seems justifiable, since the pupils of this grade receive considerable attention, these resources are decreased to approximately $1 per pupil.

Since guidance is a service designated for graduates of the high school and pupils forced to withdraw from school for gainful employment as well as those enrolled in the schools, it is impossible to determine accurately the cost of the service on a per capita basis. Numerous individuals no longer connected with the schools come to the central office of the department daily for advice along educational and vocational lines. The follow-up studies of secondary-school graduates also require considerable time. The scope of the service for which cost can not be calculated is represented by approximately 34,500 names appearing in the live-case files in the central office of the department.

Origin of the Vocational Guidance Bureau.—The Vocational Guidance Bureau of the Chicago public schools had its origin in the bureau of vocational supervision established for children by the Department of Social Investigation of the Chicago School of Civics and Philanthropy in 1910, as a result of a study by that department of the problems of truancy and nonattendance in the Chicago public schools. In the course of the study the attention of the investigators had been called to the inability of many of the children who went to work as soon as the law permitted to find satisfactory industrial placement. For example, the boys released from the parental school found industrial placement very difficult. Because of the character of the homes from which these boys came and because of the helplessness of the boys themselves when they left the parental school, advantage was taken of the opportunity offered by this investigation to advise them with reference to their choice of work and to assist them to find work when they were unwilling or unable to return to the regular day school. A small employment bureau for these boys was therefore organized in order to aid them in securing and keeping employment in Chicago.

The bureau's aim and methods during its first five years are summarized as follows in the report of the director for the school year 1916:

First.—To study industrial opportunities open to boys and girls with respect to wages and the requirements necessary to enter an occupation, the age at which beginners enter the occupations, the nature of the work, and the chances for advancement and development.

Second. To advise the children about to leave school and retain them in school when possible.

Third. When every effort to retain them in school has failed, to place in positions those children who need assistance in securing employment.

Fourth. To follow up and supervise every child who has been placed, advising him to take advantage of every opportunity for further training.

Two reports based on studies of the opportunities for employment open to children under 16 years of age in Chicago were published. More than 10,000 children were advised and assisted. A considerable majority of these were reached before they commenced to work, either just after they received their work permits or while they were still in school. The advisers held regular office hours at an increasing number of public schools for the purpose of interviewing children who planned to leave school before the completion of the regular course. Convinced by the results of their occupational studies of the meager opportunities offered children under 16, the staff aimed primarily to convince children and their parents of the value of continued education and to persuade them to remain in school or to resume their school training if they had already taken out work permits. The value of this service may be gauged by the fact that of the 3,519 children advised in the year 1914–15 who had never worked, 640 were persuaded to remain in or return to school. The need for this service may be further indicated by the fact that 1,349, or more than one-third of these children, had advanced no further in school than the sixth grade. As a necessary part of its program of keeping children in school as long as possible, the joint committee responsible for the management of the bureau entered in 1911 upon a policy of raising scholarship funds.

Since 1916, when the advisement work was taken over completely by the public schools, the program of the Vocational Guidance Bureau has followed broadly the general lines laid down during the semiprivate stage of experimentation. Its responsibilities and staff were considerably enlarged, however, by the assumption in January, 1918, of the duty of issuing employment certificates, which up to that time had been handled by the attendance department of the board of education. The extent to which the work was increased by this new responsibility is indicated by the fact that 36,605 employment certificates were issued in Chicago in the year ending June 30, 1919, 16,973 to boys and girls leaving school for work for the first time. Furthermore, the work was increased more than mere numbers would indicate by the fact that a new State child labor law which became effective July 1, 1917, embodied many new provisions and made necessary the planning of entirely new forms and administrative machinery for its enforcement. One of the most important provisions of the new law was that requiring a physical examination for all children applying for certificates. For this work a special staff of medical examiners was appointed. In September, 1919, the work was further expanded by the appointment of a staff of visiting teachers assigned to individual schools but working under the supervision of the director of the bureau. The visiting teachers were taken out of the department in 1924.

Growth of the bureau.—The growth of the bureau has been slow, beginning with three advisers in 1916. By January, 1931, the staff had been increased to 33 advisers; however, since September, 1931, 14 advisers have been transferred to teaching service in junior high schools. This drastic reduction in the number of advisers serving in the schools because of a reduced budget has seriously curtailed the effectiveness of the services of the bureau.

Of the 33 advisers in the organization before the present reduction, 7 were assigned to the central office and 26 to the schools. Thirty-two of the 50 junior and senior high schools were served by these advisers, one adviser being assigned to each of 10 senior and 9 junior high schools and the other 7 being assigned to more than 1 school.

Functions and duties of the personnel—The director.—The Director of the Vocational Guidance Bureau for the entire school system has general supervision over the work of the 33 advisers. She has defined the duties of the advisers in the schools in an attempt to standardize the work and to make the program in the schools as nearly uniform as possible. The principals of the schools in which the advisers work indicate the duties to be performed by the advisers, and the director helps to outline and organize the work of the advisers for the schools in the light of the duties which must be performed and the duties which the principals wish to have performed.

One of the distinctive contributions rendered by the director is bringing together and making available a vast amount of printed material for the use of the advisers in the schools. This material is of the following types:

(1) Occupational and educational information to be passed on to the pupils. This information is concerned with the changes in the supply and demand for workers in various fields, the training necessary for occupations, and the educational opportunities available to pupils.

(2) Posters, charts, and other graphic material for use in the schools.

(3) Lists of slides and films available.

(4) Information concerning the development of an occupational library, bibliographies on vocational guidance, and materials for an occupational library for the school.

(5) Suggestions on scheduling visits to industrial plants and business houses for groups of pupils and teachers, and procuring suitable speakers for school groups.

(6) Information to advisers concerning courses offered by the universities and colleges which are considered especially helpful to them.

(7) Information concerning new legislation affecting the schooling and employment of young people.

The central office.—The central office is organized into four divisions:

(1) Placement.

(2) Occupational studies.

(3) Employment certificates.

(4) Guidance and placement of handicapped pupils.

The placement division of the bureau.—This division is under the direction of two advisers and is organized to serve (*a*) high-school graduates and pupils dropping out of school to enter industry; (*b*) all young people subject to continuation-school requirements; and (*c*) handicapped pupils under the age of 21, especially those entering industry.

The advisers in the schools send candidates for positions to the placement division of the central office. Record cards which show the teachers' ratings of the pupils on various traits are secured by advisers for these candidates and forwarded to the placement division previous to graduation periods. Reports are made by the placement division to the advisers in the schools concerning the placements effected. Sometimes dissatisfied pupils are sent to the placement division for interviews concerning the possibilities of securing work. The division has often been able to convince these pupils of the wisdom of completing their high-school courses.

The placement division secures the records of physical examinations made by a physician on all pupils under 16 years of age who are applying to the divisions for positions. All pupils who are handicapped physically are given special consideration by this division in securing positions. This division also checks on all certificates of pupils under 16 years of age who are applying for positions. The placement division cooperates closely with the continuation schools. A teacher has been appointed in each school to cooperate with the placement division in directing pupils out of work or unsatisfactorily employed to the placement office both for registration and for the purpose of securing advice regarding employment. Preference is given to unemployed continuation-school pupils attending regularly rather than to young people who might wish to drop out of full-time school. The placement division insists that young people of continuation-school age must be in regular attendance to be eligible to its service, thus helping to maintain school attendance.

The rapid decrease in the number of positions open to children is strikingly shown by the fact that 10 years ago this division issued approximately 10,000 first full-time employment certificates, whereas during the year 1929–30 the number had decreased to 2,691, and during the year 1930–31 to 987. In spite of the rapid increase in the population of Chicago over this period, the number of employment certificates issued to minors has decreased rapidly, and at the present rate of decrease promises to reach a negligible number within a few years.

The division of occupational studies.—This division performs three general types of work:

(1) Service to the other divisions of the bureau.

(2) Collection of occupational information.

(3) Dissemination of educational and vocational information for use of advisers, teachers, and pupils in the schools.

In performing the first of these duties the division passes on the legality of the jobs to which children are to be certified, referring to information already in the files, and making special investigations as necessary. It also furnishes the medical examiner with information concerning hazards and strains involved in certain jobs. Records of accidents to minors or illness on the job are kept, and cases of illegal employment are referred to the Illinois Department of Labor.

The advisers in this division investigate practically all establishments in which children under 16 years of age are to be referred for placement. The information in the files of this division is available for reference by advisers in the placement division. The following vocational material is available in the division for the use of school principals, teachers, advisers, and pupils:

(1) *Employers' file.*—This file contains the occupational information secured in connecton with investigations for certification and placement, as well as that obtained in the course of the regular occupational studies. Several thousand establishments are included in the file and classified according to industry and occupation.

(2) *College file.*—This is an up-to-date file of college catalogues with cross file according to types of courses given.

(3) *Trade-school file.*—This is a file of literature and reports resulting from visits to business colleges and all kinds of special trade schools classified by subjects or trades taught.

(4) *Trade-association file.*—This file contains information from both union and open-shop trade organizations, from employers' organizations, and from professional groups. It includes data as to apprenticeship systems, wages, hours, etc.

(5) *Employment-agency file.*—This is an accumulation of information and testimony collected from various private employment agencies.

(6) *Library.*—This is a reference library of books and pamphlets on industries, occupations, labor conditions, vocational and educational guidance, and other special phases of education.

This material and information is disseminated through office interviews and through mimeographed and printed material distributed in the schools. From 300 to 500 requests for vocational information come to the bureau each year, by telephone, mail, or personal visit. The occupational studies are made by the advisers assigned to this division or by other advisers on the staff.

The following types of printed and mimeographed material have been prepared by this division of the Vocational Guidance Bureau: (1) Four-page bulletins dealing with occupations such as accounting, civil service, salesmanship, and stenography; (2) occupational studies of an extended character; (3) trade bulletins setting forth the requirements and opportunities in trades such as auto mechanics, bookbinding, and beauty culture; (4) leaflets giving occupational information on subjects such as earning one's way through college, show-card writing, the police service, etc.; (5) course books for use of pupils in grades 6A, 8A, and 9A; (6) special reports and manuals; (7) apprenticeship regulations for different trades providing apprenticeship training; (8) bibliographies, book lists, and pamphlet lists; (9) bulletins of information regarding leading occupations; (10) information regarding schools.

Materials of the kind indicated make possible effective guidance on the part of advisers and teachers and furnish the means of self-discovery on the part of pupils through reading. It is doubtful if the schools could assemble even a fractional portion of material, such as is represented in the types indicated, without the service of the Bureau of Vocational Guidance.

Division of employment certificates.—All employment certificates are issued through the employment certificate division of the central office. Every child applying for a certificate is interviewed by a specially qualified worker who has practical knowledge of the kinds of occupational opportunities offered in Chicago to boys and girls both with and without special training. This specialist also is acquainted with the local opportunities for continued education in different academic and practical fields. It is the duty of this adviser not only to go over the various papers presented by the child, such as the proof of age, school record, etc., to see whether or not he is legally entitled to a certificate, but also to secure from him and his parent or guardian information regarding the reasons for desiring to go to work and the financial condition of the family. The Illinois child labor law does not give permit-issuing authorities the right to refuse a work certificate to any child between 14 and 16 years of age who has completed the work of the eighth grade, but if it appears that the child will be benefited by further schooling he is urged by the adviser to return to school and the matter is discussed with his parents. If financial assistance is needed the child may be referred to one of the scholarship agencies located in the same building with the bureau.

All children receiving employment certificates come to the central bureau for physical examination. The bureau has the somewhat unusual advantage of having its physical examinations made by physicians who are members of the public-school staff and whose interests are therefore especially centered on the problem of the working child. The function of the examiners is primarily to carry out the provision of the law prohibiting the certification of children under 16 years of age for occupations for which they are not physically fit; but their work has developed other important phases from the vocational guidance point of view, such as securing the cooperation of clinics and other agencies in restoring to health children not physically fit for work, in providing supervision for children with minor physical defects who are permitted to enter industry provisionally, in instructing children with certain types of defects as to the kinds of work they can and can not undertake, in seeing that children with subnormal or psychopathic mentality are given special examination and prescribing the kind of work they are fitted for, and in directing children who have been employed in occupations physically harmful to them not to undertake the same kind of work when they change positions. The experience resulting from the reexamination of children who are changing positions, required under the Illinois law, also gives an opportunity to accumulate information regarding the effect of certain occupations and industries on young workers.

Division of guidance and placement of handicapped children.—One adviser in the central bureau is responsible for the guidance and placement of handicapped children and for adjustment to industry of children who are handicapped, either physically or mentally. The adviser carries on a vocational guidance program in the schools for crippled children and advises pupils referred from special schools and classes for the handicapped.

The adviser seeks to limit the efforts at placement to those handicapped pupils who can hope to compete with normal people when properly placed. This group has included those with orthopedic disabilities, cardiac condition, tubercular condition, the blind or partly blind, the deaf, and the high-grade mental defectives. The first step in this work is a complete medical examination of the pupils by the medical examiners of the bureau. This is followed by such special examinations as the doctors may suggest and by whatever corrective work is considered necessary. In cases of apparent subnormality, mental examination is arranged for. The next step is the determination of the placement aim, and in working toward this aim specialized training is often arranged to fit the handicapped child for a suitable vocation.

Placement is the last step. The calls from employers received by the regular placement desk are open to the adviser. In addition to this source of placement possibilities, the adviser in charge of this work has a file of employers with whom contacts have been made. The roster of the Rotarians and the Kiwanians, both of which are interested in the problem of the underprivileged child, are also open to the adviser.

Case records are kept of all children handled. These records consist of a medical card and a brief running history. Placements are ordinarily followed up within a month's time, and after that as the individual may require. A few examples of recent cases will give a more complete idea of the work of this division.

A 19-year-old boy, a graduate of a 4-year architectural drafting course, was referred to the central office by one of the schools for crippled children. The boy walked on two crutches and would have found it impossible to solicit his own job. An opportunity was secured for him in drafting with a large firm in his own neighborhood.

A deaf boy, 19 years of age, had been out of school two years doing nothing. He possessed mechanical interests and was restless and dissatisfied when idle. He was sent to the Federal Board for Vocational Rehabilitation with the request that he be entered in a trade school for a course in auto mechanics. The boy plans also to take up again his lip-reading work in which he has lost skill since leaving school.

A girl with one arm was sent to the bureau by a vocational adviser in one of the senior high schools for advice about her course. She was in the first year of high school and wished to plan her course with some definite aim toward a future vocation. Different vocations possible for a worker with one arm were considered and her course chosen in one of the occupations in which she could succeed.

A boy with an artificial leg, who possessed good mechanical ability but a rather low IQ, was finishing the eighth grade in one of the special schools for crippled children. He wished advice about his future. A special examination at the Institute for Juvenile Research was arranged. This strengthened the school report of superior mechanical but low academic ability. The examination also revealed a poor physical condition. High school was not advised and the necessity of physical rehabilitation was stressed. Plans were made for the boy to go to Arden Shore Camp for the remainder of the year to "build up" his physical condition with the possible future plan of taking trade training.

A girl from the sight-saving class was referred by the visiting teacher to the central bureau. She had completed the 4-year course in high school with emphasis on dictaphone work. She was sent to a dictaphone school for a report on her work and on the possibility of immediate placement. The school found the quality of her work good, but her speed not up to commercial requirements. She was entered in the school for additional training through the assistance of the Federal Board for Vocational Rehabilitation.

Advisers in the schools.—The advisers assigned to the various schools are specialists in vocational guidance. While they are immediately responsible to the director of the bureau, they function under the principals in organizing the plan to be carried out in the various schools and in selecting and modifying suggested procedures to conform to the school organization and needs.

The general duties performed by the advisers consist in orienting incoming pupils and in advising pupils in regard to their choice of school subjects. In performing the first duty, advisers administer tests to new pupils, visit the schools which send pupils to the high schools, and assist in the classification of entering pupils. In performing the second function the advisers aid pupils in outlining plans and in starting the differentiation of work at the proper grades in the junior and senior high schools. This work is done chiefly through the following steps: (1) Explanations of curriculums and subjects to groups of pupils either in home rooms or in other groups; (2) explanations of school offerings to parents through letter, in parent-teacher association meetings, or in special assemblies of parents; (3) assembly programs for the purpose of stimulating interest in education among the pupils; and (4) distribution and explanation of "Futures" and "Application to High School," two bulletins on educational opportunities for pupils furnished by the central office.

The advisers in the schools are responsible for individual guidance of the pupils in their charge. The advisers plan to interview each pupil before the end of his school career, although complete realization of this purpose is not often possible. The adviser will interview personally pupils whose choice of school work indicates a discrepancy between such choice and implied economic possiblities, mental possibilities, and pupils' special interests and abilities.

The advisers interview pupils who have been brought to their attention as special cases by the advisers or principals in the contributing schools. Some advisers have singled out problem cases for individual interview by means of a questionnaire used during a class group explanation of school offerings. A special effort is made to discover and interview handicapped children. Pupils in grade 9A in the junior high schools and those in grade 10A in the senior high schools who indicate that they are leaving school are interviewed personally to determine whether continued school attendance can be effected. Senior high school pupils at any point in their careers who indicate a desire for advice regarding choice of college and the articulation of high-school and college work may secure a personal conference with the advisers. For these pupils the advisers have at hand adequate reference material, college catalogues, information on college scholarship, and general reading on the meaning of college.

The work of counseling individual pupils varies to a marked degree among the individual advisers, the nature of the programs depending on the viewpoint of the adviser, the emphasis placed on the work by the principal, the type of school, and other similar factors. The advisers make strong efforts to have at least one personal interview with every pupil under their direction, but this is impossible in many schools on account of sheer numbers. Very often this one interview is held in connection with the preparation and making out of the program for the next semester or year.

In the junior high schools, counseling is given by the advisers to pupils of grades 7A and 9A in groups, and in the senior high schools entering pupils, juniors, and seniors are met by the advisers in division rooms or in available class periods. Talks are sometimes given to groups of pupils in both junior and senior high schools by business and professional men on vocational problems. No regular time has been set aside in the schools for this work; in some schools these talks are given once each semester or less frequently, and in a very few schools they are given as often as once a month. Even when instruction is given by teachers it is usually informal, irregular, and incidental to the subject matter of some regular course, such as industrial history, industrial civics, or some other course in the social sciences. Since vocational advisers have been appointed for the high schools closer cooperation with the Vocational Guidance Bureau has been established and the study of occupations as a part of the high-school curriculum has been given considerable impetus. In several schools the vocational advisers have in connection with other subjects, organized short courses in occupational information averaging about 10 lessons in length. In most of these courses each pupil is required to study at least one occupation. An outline prepared by the Vocational Guidance Bureau is followed except in one school, which uses an outline prepared by the Harvard Bureau of Vocational Guidance. Some of the courses are optional, but others reach all the pupils in the grade for which the course is given. In one school where this course is regularly given each year in connection with the study of English, every pupil is reached.

In a few schools a textbook is used in connection with the course on vocational information.

In most schools the advisers are expected to interview pupils failing in more than two subjects. This interview may be a routine procedure for pupils in their first semester in the school or in their first semester of a specialized curriculum, or it may involve special interviews for pupils whose completion of an individual subject is jeopardized.

In interviewing these pupils the procedures vary, though the end to be attained, namely, a better adjustment of the individual to the school environment, is the same. The adviser secures information from teachers concerning the pupil, his abilities and disabilities, his attitudes toward the school and teachers, and his out-of-school activities and home environment. In some cases this information is reported on a form devised for the purpose. Through an interview with the pupil this information is supplemented and the individual's attitude toward the school and school work is secured. The adviser may then give tests to determine, if possible, the location of the difficulty, or he may refer the pupil to the child study department.

The adviser may call on social agencies for special case work or treatment, and may make contact with the parents either by letter, telephone, office visit, or home call. Recommendations are made to parents and teachers and an attempt is made to help the child understand his difficulties. If a remedial class is organized in the school the pupil may be referred to it. The pupil's work is watched and followed up at subsequent periods. Registrations may be changed or, with the approval of the principal, certain subjects may be dropped or deferred or the pupil transferred to another school.

'Certain problem cases may properly be referred to the adviser by the principal, dean, or teachers. These cases may involve behavior, physical defect or poor physical condition, backward and irregular work, or poverty. Procedures are similar to those employed for failing pupils. The advisers may secure the service of the special advisers for handicapped pupils at the central bureau if such assistance is desired.

The adviser is not primarily a placement officer, but certain duties with respect to employment are naturally delegated to him. Cooperation of the advisers in the schools in securing applications of graduates and the recommendations of teachers is necessary to the functioning of the placement division in the central bureau. Pupils under 16 years are not registered with the placement division unless there is a definite understanding that the individuals will remain in school until work is secured. If pupils under 16 are recommended for placement, the adviser must first secure proof of age and the consent of parents. It is desirable that handicapped young people be sent to the special advisers for the handicapped early in their high-school careers rather than for placement at the end of the training period. Advisers may be called on to place pupils in full-time work because of the proximity of certain places of employment to the adviser's school.

Part-time employment can be handled better through the school than in any other way, and calls received at the central bureau are relayed to the schools which are able to fill them.

Since the adviser is the representative of the Vocational Guidance Bureau in the school, preliminary certification is assigned to him. The adviser must be thoroughly familiar with Laws and Regulations Affecting the Education and Work of Minors. Every effort must be made to supply pupils working full time or part time under the age of 16 with proper certificates. Pupils are required to remain in school until all papers are complete and until certificates are issued. The necessary interview with the parent may be carried out at school or the adviser may call at the pupil's home. In exceptional cases only should the parent be sent to the central bureau for interview. Proof-of-age papers and employer's statement should be in hand before the individual is sent to the Vocational Guidance Bureau.

In certification and employment policies it is imperative that the advisers carry out the practices in force at the central bureau. Unless the pupil 16 to 17 years of age is a 4-year high-school graduate, he is eligible to continuation-school enrollment when leaving school for permanent employment.

Examples of the work of individual advisers.—As has been intimated previously, the work of the individual advisers in the various schools is not standardized. The desires of the principals under whom the advisers work and the problems and situations in the schools are factors that prompt variation in advisers' programs.

In one of the technical high schools the main emphasis of the adviser is on vocational and educational guidance, although some work is done in problems of social and school adjustment. The adviser in this school has divided the work of each semester into four 5-week periods. The work of the first period is chiefly concerned with the induction of new pupils into the technical high school. Nearly 2,400 new pupils are handled in the two semesters of each year. These pupils are advised and aided in the preparation of their programs, in the details of enrollment, and in the general adjustment to the large senior high school. Special problems of the pupils coming from the junior high schools are dealt with at this time.

During the second 5-week period the adviser works through the English classes in giving group guidance to pupils concerning the election of work and the subjects required in the various curriculums. This work is done especially with the 10B classes because these pupils will be confronted with elective subjects in grade 10A. The third period of the adviser's time is taken up with the 11B English classes. The regular English teachers of these classes cooperate with the adviser in assigning, reading, and correcting vocational themes. The pupils in these classes secure information concerning various vocations through assignments made by the teachers and adviser. Themes are written from time to time concerning individual vocations selected by the pupils. In this manner the pupils secure detailed information concerning a number of occupations. A second part of the work in the third period deals with the 12A English classes. The pupils in these classes are requested to write one or two autobiographies. These themes are regarded as confidential by the adviser. They furnish a large amount of personal information concerning individual pupils which the adviser could not possibly secure in any other manner.

During the fourth 5-week period the adviser works with the individuals of the graduating class. Vocational themes are asked of some of these pupils, supplementary autobiographies of others, and all are dealt with individually, if possible, to ascertain their vocational interests and college plans. During this period also the adviser attempts to make contact with all the contributing junior high schools that send pupils to the technical high school. The offerings open to the junior high school pupils are explained, the general plan of organization is described, and in general attempts are made to aid the pupils in adjusting themselves to the new situation in the senior high school. The assistant principal and other members of the staff perform the same service in the contributing elementary schools.

The adviser in this school has individual contacts with all pupils who for any reason are withdrawing from the school. All the problem cases involving vocational or educational adjustments are sent to the adviser. Some pupils seek individual interviews with him in regard to their themes and autobiographies. However, it is not possible for the adviser to have personal contact with every pupil in the school.

The adviser performs whatever placement and follow-up work is possible. At present only a small number of boys are placed in occupations, whereas a few years ago as many as 15 boys a week were placed in part-time employment.

Special accomplishments of the adviser in this school are, among others:

(1) The vocational convention is organized under his supervision. This convention lasts one day, at which time all the third-year and fourth-year classes are dismissed and pupils are permitted to attend talks and lectures on various occupations and vocations. The convention is made to correlate with the vocational theme project in the English classes.

(2) The adviser in this school is a sponsor of the student council. The council is composed of one representative of each home room. The group meets once every two weeks. Through the council many problems of social adjustment to the school are handled, thus relieving the principal and also the adviser of many routine and petty disciplinary problems. The adviser is also responsible for the organization and program of the school chapter of the National Honor Society.

This provides an excellent opportunity to work with a select group of pupils in such matters as university requirements, scholarships, the professions, and similar projects.

(3) The third special responsibility of this adviser is research work. He has been able to find time among his many duties to carry on studies in the curriculum through which revisions in the social studies and English have been made—revisions which greatly enhance the program of guidance. Other research studies carried on by this adviser show the extent of contacts with pupils, the types of problems dealt with, and similar investigations.

It will be noted that the emphasis in this school, because of the characteristics of the school and the pupil body, is on *vocational guidance*. In contrast to this program, one carried on in a school that is not a vocational school places the emphasis on *educational guidance*. In the second case one adviser serves a junior and a senior high school located on the same school site.

The adviser in these schools has developed a set of records which carries over from the junior high school into the senior high school. The programs of the pupils leaving the junior high school are made out before they reach the upper school, thus eliminating a great amount of detail in making the transition from one school to the other. Studies have been made of the extent and causes of failure, and efforts have been put forth by the adviser and principals to reduce the number of subject failures. The adviser has organized the home-room teachers to assist in carrying out some of the details of the guidance program. Because of the large number of pupils to be handled it is impossible for the adviser to interview every pupil. However, she has selected a group of outstanding teachers in her schools to serve as individual counselors, teachers to whom pupils may go for personal contacts. A large number of graduates of the senior high school attend college; consequently the adviser lays more emphasis on the educational plans of the pupils than on vocational guidance. Advice is given in regard to the selection of college, the requirements for admission, and the selection of a curriculum in high school to meet the specific requirements. A comparatively small amount of attention is given to purely vocational counseling.

The foregoing illustrations show clearly that the programs of individual advisers vary to a marked degree, the different emphases depending on the functions which the principals of the schools wish to have performed, the character of the pupil enrollment, and the specific purposes of the schools.

Cost of the guidance service.—The Bureau of Vocational Guidance in the Chicago schools was established to serve all the pupils in the entire school system. The occupational studies, the printed and mimeographed materials, as well as the services for physical examinations and certificating of pupils, are available to the teachers and principals of all the schools. However, in actual practice the services of the bureau apply to the pupils in the high schools and in the upper grades of the elementary schools almost exclusively. In computing the cost of the guidance service, only the pupils who are directly benefited by the services of the bureau are included. The total appropriation for the Bureau of Vocational Guidance for salaries and office expenses for the year 1931 amounted to $150,372. The enrollment in the grades above the sixth—the grades in which the services of the bureau are used almost exclusively—was in that year 177,465. The cost per pupil for the guidance service, then, was a little less than 85 cents.

Another method of determining the cost of the guidance program in Chicago is to include in the calculations the salaries of the advisers serving in the secondary schools and the number of pupils actually being served by these advisers. The salaries of the 24 advisers for the year 1931 was $69,000, and the enrollment in the 29 junior and senior high schools in which these advisers served was 90,516. The salary cost for the advisory service in these secondary schools was approximately 76 cents per pupil.

In either case it is seen that the per pupil cost of the guidance service provided in the secondary schools of the Chicago public-school system is very low.

Evaluation.—The Bureau of Vocational Guidance has been recently evaluated in the survey of the Chicago public schools, the findings of which are both commendatory and critical. The activities of the vocational advisers are appraised as follows:

The reports of the various advisers in the secondary schools of Chicago indicate that the proper functions of guidance have not been carefully delineated. The program in some schools is radically different in many respects from the program in other schools. Such variations as are demanded by difference in localities in which the schools are situated are to be commended. Variations that lie outside the reasonable scope of guidance activity are open to question. There seems to be more or less uncertainty in Chicago concerning which guidance responsibilities are properly the function of the home-room teacher and which are properly the function of advisers. In some instances there is an overlapping of activities allotted to the dean of girls, the dean of boys, the principal, or the teachers. The practice of maintaining advisers in only approximately half of the schools may be largely responsible for some of the apparent confusion.[1]

The inadequacy of the service of the bureau and the recommendation of the survey staff for meeting the problem are indicated in the following statement:

The present staff of the bureau of vocational guidance is inadequate to provide trained advisers for all the junior and senior high schools. At the present time 13 of the 25 high schools and 21 of the 27 junior high schools have no special advisers assigned by the general office of the work. In some of the schools, teachers, heads of departments, or assistant principals are advising pupils in regard to vocational programs. In view of the present economic situation and the remote possibility of securing a central office staff large enough to provide this service for all of the junior and senior high schools, it would be desirable to organize extension courses in guidance as an aid to the teachers or assistants in the junior and senior high schools who are advising pupils in regard to their educational and vocational programs. The principal of each junior and senior high school should recognize the importance of guidance as a necessary school service and cooperate in planning a training program for those doing the work in their schools. A decentralized guidance service would result in the schools' assuming a more direct responsibility for the work.

The central office should continue its special studies and make available to those doing the advising in the schools material in regard to vocations, training opportunities, and other helpful information. The central office should also assume responsibility for the planning and general supervision of the guidance work in the junior and senior high schools.[2]

---

[1] Strayer, G. D., *and staff.* Report of the Survey of the Schools of Chicago, Ill., vol. II, p. 123, 1932.

[2] Ibid., vol. III, p. 221.

The recommendation of the survey staff with regard to the reorganization of the Bureau of Vocational Guidance, if carried out, will greatly alter its character.

The activities of the bureau of vocational and educational guidance are confined to junior and senior high schools, and in these is limited to only about half of the schools. In the scope, variety, and quality of its work in placement, guidance, certificating, and dissemination of information, this bureau seems to have rendered a noteworthy service. It is deserving of much commendation and more generous financial support. The tendency to centralize such services along administrative lines, rather than along supervisory and service lines, must be carefully avoided if the work of this bureau is to be of greatest value to the Chicago schools.[3]

[3] Strayer, G. D., *and staff*. Report of the Survey of the Schools of Chicago, Ill., vol. V, p. 83.

CHAPTER VI : CASE REPORT ON PROVIDENCE

Organization of guidance.—Guidance in the schools of Providence is an integral part of the administration and curriculum of the school system. It is regarded as an aspect of education which has grown in prominence with the increasing tendency toward specialization on the part of the school. The departmental organization of the modern city school and the specialized functions of its personnel place the child in the hands of many persons in the course of his progress through the school. Since each person sees only a small part of the child and for only a short time, the responsibility for his many-sided development is scattered, no one in particular assuming a definite responsibility for the finished product.

To meet the condition described, the schools of Providence have in recent years emphasized guidance as a function of education and have developed an organization designed to compensate the individual child for the diffusion of responsibility on the part of the school staff.

An assistant superintendent is charged with the responsibility of coordinating the various departments of the school system, to the end that responsibility for the development of the individual pupil is brought to a focus. The assistant superintendent acts as a supervisor to aid the principals and counselors to improve the counseling service and programs. A staff of six class counselors, organized in each of the secondary schools, accepts definite responsibility for the counseling and guidance of each individual pupil. The organization of the guidance responsibility has resulted in the lay-out shown in Figure 8.

Functions of the Department of Personnel Research and Guidance.—The functions of the organization designated as the Department of Personnel Research and Guidance are threefold: (1) Personnel research; (2) orientation; (3) counseling.[1]

By personnel research is meant the scientific study of the individual with the view of contributing to his adjustment.

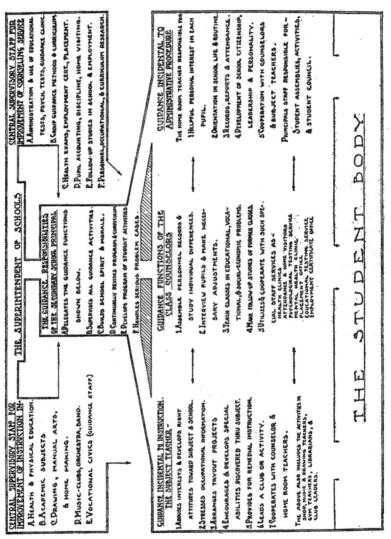

FIGURE 8.—Organization of guidance in a secondary school of Providence, R. I.

The activities of the staff members in carrying on personnel research are:

---

[1] These functions and the activities described under each are indorsed in a conference report prepared at Harvard University and published in the Junior-Senior High School Clearing House, 5:21-26, September 1930.

1. Continuous records of attendance, health, achievement, interests, personal data.

2. Records of periodic surveys of intelligence, educational tests, aptitudes, prospects.

3. Studies of pupil adjustment in classification and choice of electives.

4. Studies in articulation and pupil turnover.

5. Basic data for construction of the school program.

6. Studies for a redefinition of school and curricular objectives.

7. Psychological and psychiatric examinations (provided the services of a trained worker are available).

8. Records, pamphlets, and catalogues of schools for further education.

The second function, orientation, is used in the sense of adjustment to the common needs of the pupil. It is carried on through group instruction and conferences by a trained counselor, who understands the common problems of pupils. The desired results are achieved for a large proportion of the pupils through educational and occupational information, the establishment of habits, and the development of attitudes and ideals, all of which, according to the views of the Department of Personnel Research and Guidance, can be realized as well or better through dealing with pupils in groups than by dealing with them individually. The following activities are considered to belong to the function of orientation as defined:

1. How to study, how to budget one's time, how to succeed in school, how to take examinations.

2. How to use the guidance library.

3. How to choose electives, colleges, other educational opportunities, vocational education.

4. Vocational opportunities, the study of occupations, local employments, apprenticeship, evening schools.

5. How to meet problems of personal and social relations, student legislature or forum, case conferences, student council, school civic problems, etc.

Counseling, the third function, is regarded as an act of advising or deliberating together. It is carried on by means of the interview between counselor and individual pupil.

The interview may be sought by the pupil or the counselor. In either case the function of counseling presupposes systematic effort on the part of the school to utilize the information collected through personnel research to prevent individual maladjustment and to effect adjustments not possible to obtain through group advisement. The activities of counseling practiced in the secondary schools of Providence are the following:

1. Leaving school to enter employment (interviews with pupil and parent—employment service and issue of work certificate).

2. Checking unwise choices of electives.

3. Special problems of health, absence, failure, transfer, and social adjustment.

4. Home visits and conferences with parent.

5. Educational and vocational plans.

6. Periodic check-up on educational progress.

7. Possible changes in the school curriculum and program which concern teachers, department heads, and the principal.

8. Follow-up reports of graduates and of employed pupils in evening or continuation schools.

Selection of counselors.—The technical character of the functions of guidance requires the selection of persons with special training and personal qualifications for the work. The selection in Providence is made from teachers, because the counselor must teach and has the rating of a teacher. Individuals are chosen who have undertaken to prepare for counseling through summer or extension courses and who have manifested a personal interest in the work. The appointment of a teacher as a counselor in a given school merely means a transfer from one field of teaching to another with the added duties of personnel research and counseling. (See Fig. 9.[2])

Further training of counselors is undertaken through supervision after the individual receives appointment. The in-service training is carried on through the head counselor of the school, the principal, the assistant superintendent in charge of guidance, and other members of the Department of Personnel Research and Guidance.

[2] Fig. 9 was prepared by Richard D. Allen and Lester J. Schloerb.

The plan presented in Figure 10 indicates the method of securing continuous training for counselors. The plan insures for each counselor a 3-year training in all special guidance activities. The first series of conferences are interschool, with counselors of the same grade in each school and

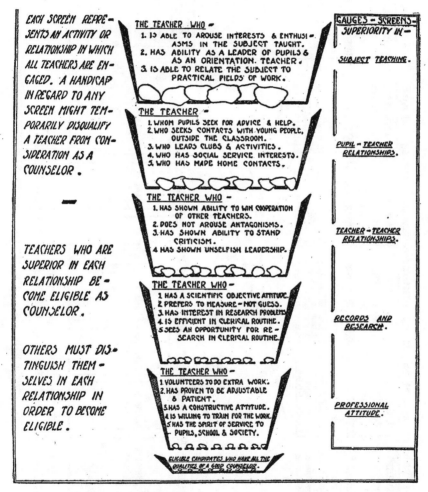

FIGURE 9.—Five screens for the selection of counselors

the staff specialist from the central office representing the designated field of training. These six conferences are held during alternate weeks. During intervening weeks the conferences are intraschool. In these the counselors and other workers in each school meet for training conferences to discuss, evaluate, and put into operation any valuable findings from the interschool conferences. It should be noted further that as counselors move up into their next grade they move

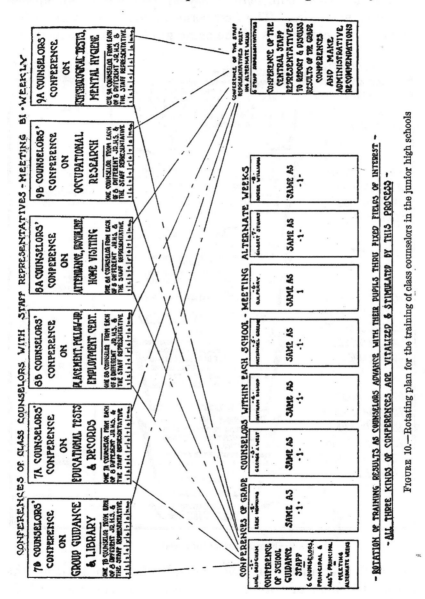

FIGURE 10.—Rotating plan for the training of class counselors in the junior high schools

up to the next field of training. This makes possible continuous rotation of the training activites.

Scope of counselor's duties.—The following program has been evolved for counselors in the secondary schools of Providence:

1. Of a 25-period load per week, each of the class advisers is given one period a day for individual conferences for each 200 to 300 pupils in his class.

2. Whenever possible, advisers are relieved of home-room duties in order to assist in home-room programs, to confer with other teachers and with parents, and to meet committees of pupils.

3. The adviser is given an entire grade of pupils for whom he is to be responsible during their entire school course.

4. The adviser teaches the course on occupations to all of the sections of his grade for one period each week for three years. Thus he is responsible for the background of occupational information which all children need. He can study their reactions to occupational interests over a period of three years.

5. The adviser conducts a pupils' forum for one period each week in each section of his grade. Problems of personal and social relations are discussed, as well as choices of electives, school activities, and community problems. Thus the adviser has an opportunity to study individual social reactions. The class is often conducted by the case-conference method.

6. The adviser will have less than 10 hours per week scheduled in other school subjects. The chief adviser, or head of the department, is allowed a period each day for supervision and may be allowed another period per day for the continuous study of the program of the school.

Instruction in occupations in the junior high school.—The vocational orientation of the pupil is accomplished in part through class instruction in occupations. Pupils in grades 7–9 receive instruction two periods per week. The classes are taught by the counselors, each counselor being assigned, as a rule, to the classes in which are enrolled the pupils regarding whom the counselor is expected to carry on personnel research and with whom individual counseling is to be given.

The course in occupations deals with occupational information and the orientation of the pupil to important problems in occupations. The pupil is provided with the opportunity in the course to acquire both extensive and intensive knowledge of local occupations and to learn of the present opportunities for employment, the nature of the demands made upon a worker, and the advantages and disadvantages in the different occupations. Orientation is provided through instruction in how to choose an occupation, how to apply for a position, how to go to work in a position, etc.

Perfunctory consideration of occupations and occupational problems is avoided by assigning the work to the qualified counselors instead of to regular teachers with limited occupational knowledge, little interest in the course, and lack of specific training for the work.

Educational orientation in the junior high school.—Part of the class-period time in the seventh and eighth grades set aside for guidance is utilized by the counselor to aid the pupils in becoming properly oriented to the junior high school, the specific objectives of the counselor being to help the pupil understand and appreciate his new surroundings, to assist him in acquiring habits of independent study, to guide him in planning his education, and to aid him in seeing beyond immediate school problems the broader issues of which present choices are only a part.

Case conferences.—Some of the periods reserved for group instruction are used by the counselors for case conferences. The case material is previously prepared with care, and the method employed by the counselors is that of the conference technique.

The counselor selects a case believed to be typical for a majority of the pupils in the group; that is, the majority of the pupils are believed to recognize in the case a problem similar to problems in their own experience. The background of experience constitutes the preparation for the consideration of the case. Without such a background the method in most instances is ineffective. The case chosen should also challenge the intelligence of the pupils. If the solution of the case is obvious, too difficult, far-fetched, or involves too fine a distinction, more harm than good may result from the conference. The material should also be prepared with a view of avoiding rambling and aimless discussion.

The case material in use in Providence has been prepared with the idea of avoiding such weakness. The cases were prepared, used, and revised in the light of criticisms received from the counselors. They are believed to constitute at present very valuable material for group use in moral and ethical guidance, provided that the technique of conducting the case conference is understood and skillfully executed by the conference leader.

The following case illustrates the kind of problem selected for conferences and the questions used to stimulate discussion on the part of the pupils. The case is read by some pupil at the request of the class leader or counselor, and each question is considered until a majority of the group appears to accept an answer.

"She Was Picking on Me"

Betty is told by the study teacher to leave the study hall and report to the office. Betty can not understand why she has been sent out. She hasn't whispered, she hasn't passed a note, she hasn't broken any schoolroom law so far as she knows. In fact, she was not doing anything. She was a few minutes late in reporting to the study period because the cooking teacher detained several of the girls whose kitchens did not look very neat. But then, Miss B gave her an admit slip to study hall. So what more can Miss S expect? When she reached her study desk she found that she had her literature book instead of her algebra book, which she needed, and so she asked and obtained permission to go to her locker room to exchange books. She hurried right back. She did not waste a minute on the way. She was just ready to settle down to work when she discovered that the paper on which she wrote her algebra assignment was not in her book. She remembered immediately that she had loaned it to Sarah F. She noticed that Miss S was none too gracious when she asked if she might speak to Sarah about it. But she wasn't to blame if Sarah had not returned it. Well, once more she was ready to begin her work, when snap! went the point on her only pencil. She looked up. Miss S was watching, just ready to "pick on her," and without allowing Betty to make one word of explanation, said, "Leave the room. Report at the office."

1. Why do you think Betty was sent out?
2. Should she have been sent out?
3. Was Miss S unfair? Was she just waiting to "pick on" Betty?
4. What are study periods for?
5. Is "doing nothing" permissible?
6. How much had Betty accomplished?
7. Is time worth anything?
8. How should a pupil plan to use his study period? Why?
9. What preparations should a pupil make for a study period?

Personnel records and reports.—The Providence school system maintains excellent continuous records for pupils from the time of admission to graduation. The individual records are cumulative in character and are transferred with the pupil from grade to grade and school to school. Personnel charts are also kept for each class, showing the distribution of the pupils according to chronological age, mental age, intelligence quotient, and achievement level. The data thus made available in the records for counselors facilitate classification.

A permanent record is also kept of the scores made by each pupil on standardized achievement tests, psychological tests, and changes in the development of personal traits and qualities, such as courtesy, initiative, self-reliance, reliability, disposition, and general appearance. Other data recorded on visible record forms are physical and health status, special interests and abilities, and family history. A questionnaire to the pupil collects detailed personal data impossible to incorporate in the permanent record. The data on the questionnaire are tabulated by the counselors for their pupils and are filed in the cumulative folders of the individual pupils.

The records make possible personnel research by the counselors both for classes and individuals, and enable them to offer counsel and guidance with a background of knowledge and understanding.

Guidance clinics.—Guidance clinics are held at the central office of the Education Department for the diagnosis of problem cases found by the counselors in the schools. The specialists of the education staff participate in the clinics and give advice regarding the treatment of the cases. The organization of the Providence schools facilitates such services, which may be had at the request of the school principal, counselor, or parent. The extent of the service of the clinics is indicated by the number of cases studied during the school year 1930–31, which was 305.

Incidental guidance.—Each counselor is provided with bulletins prepared in the central office for the use of school bulletin boards in offering incidental guidance to pupils. The systematic use of these bulletins enriches the possibilities of reaching some pupils through the incidental means. Figure 11 illustrates the kind of bulletins used.

Placement service.—An effective central placement service is maintained in the Providence school system. The records of placements are kept on file in the central office and placement contacts are made by the supervisor of guidance and placement in the Department of Research and Guidance. Many placements are also made through the shop instructors in the trade school, who use one-half day each week in making contacts with employers as a means of finding placements for their pupils. Counselors in the different schools keep in touch with pupils 15 to 16 years of age who are employed part time or on unskilled jobs. The placements made through the schools average about 1,000 per year in normal times.

NO SKILLED TRADE IS OPEN TO YOU UNTIL YOU ARE AT LEAST SIXTEEN YEARS OF AGE

Don't Waste Your Time in the Meanwhile

GO TO HIGH SCHOOL
It Will Open All the Trades and
Professions to You

FIGURE 11.—A guidance bulletin for posting on a bulletin board

Follow-up studies.—Follow-up studies are made of high-school graduates at intervals of 1, 3, and 5 years. The studies are made by the counselors and are tabulated for the schools in the central office. Semester reports are required of the counselors for pupils leaving school during the semester, including statement of cause of withdrawal. The data are sent to the principals and are used by administrative officers in the reorganization of programs of study and the administrative policies of the different schools. Each junior high school counselor also makes follow-up studies of pupils 1, 2, and 3 years after completion of the ninth grade.

Cost of guidance.—The net cost of guidance per pupil in Providence as estimated by the assistant superintendent in charge of guidance for a standard junior or senior high school is about $2.50 per year. This is based on the time of six class counselors used in individual counseling of pupils.

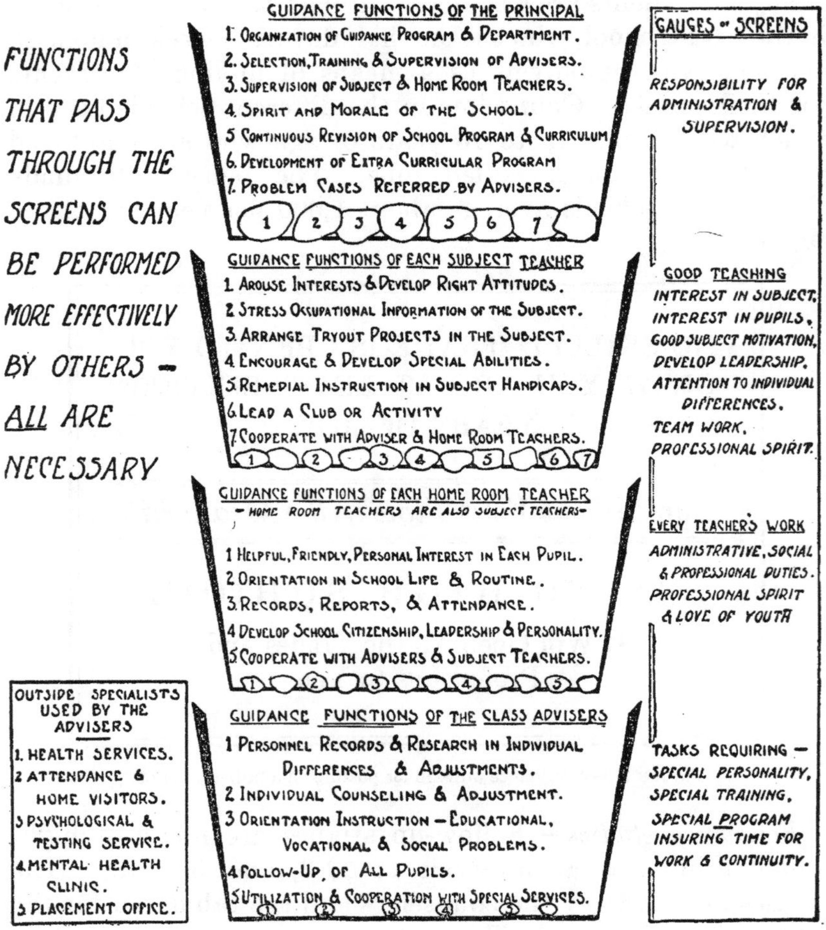

FIGURE 12.—Screens for the guidance functions of principal, subject teachers, home-room teachers, and class advisers

If other activities which are charged to instruction, namely, instruction in occupations and case conferences, are allocated to guidance, the net cost would be increased by approximately $7 a pupil per year. Since the time given to occupations and the class conferences is taken from other subjects, the time used for these activities would probably be absorbed by the other subjects if guidance were dropped. The first figure for individual counseling, therefore, appears more nearly than the second to approximate the cost of guidance in the secondary schools of Providence. No saving in overhead would be effected if guidance were discontinued, as the time given by administrative officers to guidance is allocated to instruction on the ground that guidance is really a function of the educative process. The work of class counselors in no way interferes with the guidance functions of subject teachers or home-room teachers. This may be seen from Figure 12,[3] which shows the specific guidance functions of the principal, subject teachers, home-room teachers, and class advisers. The advisers perform only those functions that can not be performed effectively by teachers and administrative officers.

[3] Prepared by Richard D. Allen and Lester J. Schloerb.

CHAPTER VII : CASE REPORT ON CINCINNATI

Historical development in Cincinnati.—The Vocation Bureau of the Cincinnati public schools was organized under private funds in 1911, and later became a joint enterprise of the public schools and the local Council of Social Agencies. Its purpose was the study of child labor in the city under the provisions of the child labor law of 1910. This law gave the superintendent of schools legal supervision of children leaving school to enter industry at 14 years of age. The employment certificate office was transferred to the new bureau, and the psychological laboratory and a department for home visiting were established, thus making possible the collection of data and the scientific study of young beginners in industry. The work of the bureau for the first four years was centered on two projects—the administration of the employment certificate office and an intensive investigation of the working children. Following this, in 1915, a placement office was organized in the bureau; in 1918 the administration of the scholarship fund of the Council of Defense was taken over; in 1919, supervision of mental testing in the juvenile court and, in 1920, certain functions of the juvenile court were assigned to the bureau; in 1920, the attendance department of the school census was made a part of the bureau; in 1921, the bureau assumed the responsibility for the preparation of pamphlets on occupations for use in the schools; in 1926, the division of individual adjustments, which later became known as the visiting teacher division, was organized; in 1927, to the work in occupational research were added classes in occupations and individual counseling, and these three functions became the Division of Occupational Research and Counseling.

Present organization.—The Vocation Bureau is now organized in five divisions, with the functions indicated briefly in Figure 13. The only changes in organization have been the discontinuance of the placement office (which has since been taken over by the municipal Department of Public Welfare). The Division of Occupational Research and Counseling has functional responsibility for the guidance of pupils in the secondary schools, although the other divisions contribute both directly and indirectly to the guidance work. Certain types of cases must be handled by more than one

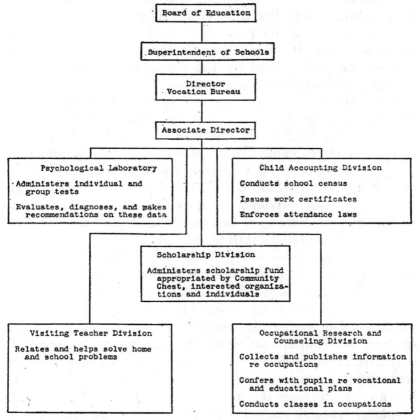

FIGURE 13.—Organization and functions of the Vocation Bureau, Cincinnati, Ohio

division of the bureau. All divisions cooperate closely, with each contributing its particular service in the solution of difficult problems. Where the major problem, however, falls within one special division, the worker in that division assumes special responsibility for the case.

The bureau as a whole and through all its divisions is in constant cooperation with the social agencies of the city and with all the community's resources for treatment. As a public-school activity, with the community-wide contacts of the school and its hold on the family through the children, it has an unequaled strategic position for the discovery and diagnosis of mental, physical, and social ills. Called upon by the schools for aid in the solution of all kinds of educational problems, the bureau not only enlists the activities of outside agencies but in turn the records and the staff of the bureau are constantly consulted by the other agencies.

The service that the Vocation Bureau renders to the social agencies of the city is particularly appropriate as a recognition of the part played by the Community Chest in contributing to the bureau's support.

When the bureau was organized in 1911, its entire budget ($5,000) was provided from private funds (the Schmidlapp Bureau). By 1922 its budget had increased to $60,000, of which two-thirds came from public funds and the remainder from private sources (the Community Chest and the Schmidlapp Bureau). In 1930–31, all but 7 per cent of its budget ($161,954) was provided from public funds. The entire budget of the Division of Occupational Research and Counseling is now supplied out of school funds.

Staff and functions.—The staff of the Division of Occupational Research and Counseling consists of the director, seven counselors, and three clerks. The counselors spend approximately half of their time in conferring with individual pupils, a fourteenth in teaching classes in occupations, a seventh in occupational research, and the remaining two-sevenths in conferring with teachers, principals, and representatives of social agencies (including other divisions of the bureau) concerning the problems of individual pupils, in preparing special projects for the class in occupations, in making contacts with parents, and in arranging trips for pupils, etc. The counseling and class work are conducted in the schools to which each counselor is assigned; the occupational research is carried on in the field, using the central office of the division as headquarters for this activity.

Counselors are assigned to regular duties in counseling in grades 8 and 9 (and for selected work with grades 10, 11, and 12) in three 6-year high schools, in grades 8 and 9 in three junior high schools, and in grade 8 in 18 elementary schools. The work in these schools consists chiefly in teaching 10 lessons on occupations to eighth-grade and ninth-grade[1] pupils and in counseling with each pupil at least once during the year regarding educational and vocational plans.

The schools included in the program were selected after conference with the superintendent, principals, and director of the Vocation Bureau because they offered special opportunities for service. The emphasis has been on the selection of schools in a small related area where a more thorough program can be carried than if the services of the small staff included the entire school system.

The first definite counseling program was introduced in 1927 in two junior high schools as demonstration centers. The functions of the division as stated by the director are threefold: (1) Instruct classes in occupations; (2) counsel with individuals regarding educational and vocational plans; (3) carry on occupational research.

The Division of Occupational Research and Counseling emphasizes—

(1) An understanding of the individual child and his problems, based on a careful study of such material as is available from the psychological laboratory, the school grades, teachers' estimates, social agencies, etc., as well as conferences with the child himself.

(2) A knowledge of the world of occupations and the related problems gained by each counselor through her contact with industry and business, as she conducts field investigations and makes the results of these available for other counselors. Each counselor spends part of one day each week in occupational research, which amounts to approximately 30 full days each year.

The program has grown slowly but very steadily, confining itself to a definitely related area rather than spreading in early years to include the entire school system. One counselor is in charge of the counseling program at each of the three 6-year high schools. There is also one counselor in

---

[1] The classes (or group conferences) in the ninth grades of the 3 junior-senior high schools range from 5 to 6 instead of 10.

each of the two junior high schools, while the remaining two counselors are in charge of the work in one small junior high school and in the eighth grades of the 18 elementary schools included in the program. One of the counselors also holds special office hours at the central office, when boys and girls from any of the schools not included in the program at present and from social agencies may be referred for vocational counseling. Each year the program has grown, and it is hoped that in the years to come it will continue to grow until the service is available in equal measure for all pupils.

Classes in occupations.—The classes in occupations (or group conferences on occupations) in the schools participating in the guidance program of the division are taught by the vocational counselors. The contact thus made by the counselor with the pupils in groups affords an excellent *entree* for the subsequent individual conferences.

The purposes of the lessons in the eighth grade are: (1) to broaden the occupational outlook of the pupils, (2) to help the pupils to realize the interrelations of the various groups of occupations, and (3) to provide them with sufficient occupational information to choose their school courses and future vocations. Much attention is given by the counselor to a survey of important occupations. Slides and pictures are used to vitalize the work, and notebooks are prepared by the pupils, illustrated by pictures and statements bearing on the occupations studied. Time is also given to the discussion of educational plans for the future.

In the ninth grade the counselor aims (1) to impress upon the pupils the importance of adequate occupational information as a basis for intelligent educational and vocational choices, (2) to help them to develop methods of studying and evaluating an occupation which will be of assistance in later life, and (3) to encourage them to think definitely about two or three occupations for which they may wish to prepare and to supply them with the necessary preparation for such thinking.

Individual conferences.—After the class work on occupations is completed, which is usually done during the first half of the school year, the counselor plans an individual conference with each pupil in the eighth and ninth grades

(and selected pupils in the upper grades) regarding his
choice of school courses and vocation. Before sending for
the pupil the counselor will have secured and studied the
following information concerning him:

1. A schedule filled out by the pupil at the time of the first meeting
of the class in occupations which presented certain aspects of his home,
and family relations, his special interests and activities, and, if he had
thought about the question, his plans for the future.

2. A form filled out by the teacher on which she estimated any
special characteristics, abilities, or weaknesses of the pupil and gave
helpful information that she may have had concerning him or his
home.

3. Information based on the cumulative school record which had
followed the child from class to class since his enrollment in kinder-
garten, and which often contains valuable information concerning his
school record, family, and special abilities.

4. A current school record on which were reported the pupil's grades
in the various subjects as listed on his report card.

5. Results of psychological tests and facts and interpretations concerning them.

6. Data from social agencies which were known to be interested in
the pupil or his family.

7. The counselor's record of any previous conference or conferences
with the pupil.

The vocational conferences provide an opportunity for the
counselor to discuss with each individual pupil the problems
that directly affect him and which may have an important
bearing on his educational and vocational plans. The
presence or absence of some definite thought for the future,
the talents and inclinations which affect a young person's
choice of career, and the necessity for adequate and suitable
school training for the vocation chosen are considered. The
vocational counselor gives the pupil additional information
concerning occupations in which he definitely expresses an
interest and those in which she believes his special abilities
might lead to success. She tells him of the various schools
which would prepare him for these different types of work
and urges him to talk over his tentative plans with his parents and to be prepared at the end of the school year, with
a more carefully thought out plan for his future school work
and his occupational goal. The counselor sends a letter to
the parents indicating the tentative plans, suggesting that
these be discussed at home, that the parents send word to

the counselor of their approval or disapproval, and that, if possible, they come to the school to confer with the counselor concerning special problems. The counselor at all times in her work with the pupils stresses the importance of a broad outlook on occupations, and only when it is absolutely necessary does she encourage the boy or girl to narrow his vocational choice. The counselor also is careful never to impose her plan upon the pupil, but to help him by means of special information and frank discussion to make his own plan for the future.

The conferences are of long enough duration for the counselor to gain the child's confidence and become acquainted with the various problems which may affect his future. The conferences are based on a knowledge of the child and of the facts, made available through a careful system of record keeping, which leads to an understanding of each individual's problems. Any special problems discovered are referred to specialists in various fields. Close cooperation with the social agencies of the city (such as the family case-working agencies, the juvenile court, etc.) has resulted in many of these agencies referring for counseling all children among their active cases who fall within certain age groups. In each case the agency sends a helpful record of information concerning the child whom they are referring for counsel. Through the counseling program the vocational counselor gives information to the child as it is needed, helps him to secure valuable experiences, assists him to interpret the information and experiences, and aids him in discovering his own interests and abilities. The counselor encourages the child to work out his own plans and make his own selections, and never attempts to force another's decision upon him. Above all, the counselor constantly strives to help the pupil develop a method of thinking which will assist him to meet his present and future problems, especially those which pertain to the preparation for, choice of, and adjustment in his future part in the world's work. Thus he may enter and succeed in the occupation which will make possible for him a happy and useful life as an individual and as a citizen and through which he may render his greatest service to the community.

The Cincinnati program of individual counseling especially emphasizes the following features:

(1) Vocational counseling conducted as a more thorough program in a smaller area rather than a less thorough program in a more extensive area.[2]

(2) Careful correlation with such special services as those offered by psychologists, visiting teachers, scholarship committees, attendance officers, and special social agencies.

(3) Trained vocational counselors who have a background of, and constant contact with, industry and business as they continue through visits and interviews to secure occupational information.

(4) Vocational counseling which emphasizes the importance of adequate records and is based on a knowledge of the child and facts which lead to an understanding of each pupil's individual problems.

(5) Individual conferences of long enough duration so that the child may not feel hurried and the counselor may have an opportunity to gain his confidence and become acquainted with the various problems which will affect his educational and occupational choice.

(6) Vocational counseling which aims to discover any special problem needing attention and which refers such a problem to the worker specializing in that field.

(7) Vocational counseling which aims to help each child make and carry out the plans best suited to his needs, interests, and abilities. For some this means college preparation and the professions; for a much larger group, high school or vocational school and the occupations to which they lead; and for others, immediate employment.

(8) Educational guidance which aims to broaden the child's outlook upon occupations and only encourages him to narrow his choice when that is urgently desirable.

(9) Vocational counseling which encourages the child to work out his own plans and make his own decisions, and which never attempts to force a decision upon him.

Pupils are seen for one conference unless there are special problems necessitating a second conference, and in a few cases, even a third or fourth. Pupils above the ninth grade in the three senior high schools participating in the division's program are interviewed and advised at the request of the individual pupil or an administrative officer of the school, or may have been selected by the counselor as in special need of a follow-up conference.

Evaluation of individual conferences in terms of types of pupils counseled.—The value of the individual conferences can be judged in terms of the types of pupils interviewed by

---

[2] The number of schools included in the program has gradually increased from 2 to 24.

the counselors.   The following classification is based on the total cases counseled in the different schools:

(1) Those who have made no plan, or only a vague or partial plan, who need help and encouragement in working out their problems and discovering the occupation which they wish to enter, and who need information about how best to prepare for it.

(2) Those who have made a plan unsuited to their abilities; for example, the child who has not the mental capacity to complete high school but who wishes to become a doctor, or the child, superior in intelligence and mechanical ability, who is satisfied with his plan to begin work when 16 and enter one of the skilled trades. The first boy, the dull child, a poor and unwilling student, is usually helped by a discussion of difficulties of the long period of training which the doctor must successfully complete; the second boy, of superior intelligence and mechanical ability, is usually helped by a discussion of the wider occupational opportunities open to graduates from a college of engineering.   Both are encouraged to make new and more suitable plans in the light of these discussions.

(3) Those who have no realization of what their chosen occupation involves; for example, the boy who chose patternmaking, yet disliked his class in woodwork and received his poorest grade in that subject. He had heard from some one that patternmaking was a good trade and was planning to take a school course that would prepare him for it.

(4) Those who have made a decision, forced upon them by economic necessity; for example, the specially able and ambitious children who would have to leave school unless they were referred for scholarships or aided by some social agency.

(5) Those who have made plans suited to their interests and abilities but whose families try to interfere and force another plan—*their* plan—upon the child; for example, the boy who loved his commercial subjects, in which he was doing excellent work, while he disliked his shop classes, of which printing was one, and in which he was receiving his lowest marks.   His family were insisting that he give up his plan to complete the commercial course in the senior high school with bookkeeping in view and that he enter a trade course which would prepare him to become a printer.   In this case a conference between the vocational counselor and family was necessary to help them see the wisdom of letting the boy carry out his own plans.

(6) Those who seem to have made a wise choice of occupation but who have no idea how or where to secure the necessary preparation.

(7) Those who plan to leave school, who have been receiving poor grades and have lost interest in school and who, through assistance in making an occupational plan, begin to realize the importance of further school work and the value of school work well done.

(8) Those who are drifters and failures in school and seem unable or unwilling to profit from school work.   These are encouraged and assisted to find immediate employment which will stimulate them in establishing better habits.

(9) Those who have special personal problems and who need help in making adjustments before success in any occupation may be possible.

(10) Those who have made good plans in regard to their occupational choice and training, with whom a conference may scarcely seem to be necessary, but who are strengthened in their plans and given important information concerning their choice of occupation and the possibilities for training.

Occupational research.—The Vocation Bureau believes that one essential of a vocational counseling program is a solid foundation of accurate and up-to-date educational and occupational information which may be drawn upon by the vocational counselors for work with their classes in occupations and for vocational conferences with individual pupils. In order to secure this information, to keep it at the maximum of accuracy, to provide each counselor with contacts with business, industry, and the professions, and to develop the point of view which such contacts make possible, the counselors spend approximately 30 days a year in the gathering and preparation of new data and in the revision of old information. In the process are included visits to industrial establishments and interviews with employers, managers, and workers, as well as with technical authorities, in the various business and professional fields. The counselors study and analyze the information which they thus secure and prepare it so that it may be used by other counselors, by teachers, and pupils. This material now analyzes more than 300 occupations and training centers and is prepared in three forms: (1) Printed pamphlets; [3] (2) simple mimeographed descriptions, especially for the use of children; and (3) detailed occupational analyses filed in loose-leaf notebook form for the use of all counselors, who thus have in each school a definite fund of up-to-date information concerning occupations and the schools and special training centers which offer preparation for these.

The printed vocational pamphlets, descriptive of occupations in Cincinnati and the economic factors involved, frankly discuss the advantages and disadvantages. The primary purpose of these studies is to furnish teachers and counselors

[3] These include an Introduction to the Study of Occupations, The Shoe Industry in Cincinnati, The Garment Industry in Cincinnati, The Metal Industries in Cincinnati, The Banking Industry in Cincinnati, Street-Railway Transportation in Cincinnati, The Post-Office in Cincinnati, The Paper-Box Industry in Cincinnati, the Policeman in Cincinnati, and The Printing Industry in Cincinnati.

information and supplementary text materials for their use in discussing with their classes the different ways in which people earn a living in the local community. The pamphlets are intended for use in the junior high school grades and above. The introductory pamphlet contains suggestions for teaching occupational information.

It has been found that one of the most effective ways of helping the pupil to work out a satisfactory educational and vocational plan is to discuss with him frankly the definite facts concerning any occupation in which he may be interested, considering it in the light of its advantages and disadvantages and of his special interests and abilities.

The average program of activities of a counselor.—The scope of the activities of a counselor is shown quantitatively in Table 1.

TABLE 1.—*Average program of a counselor for the school year 1931–32*

Activity:	Number
Days engaged in occupational research	29
Number of occupational outlines prepared	24
Class periods taught in occupations	160
Total number of pupils counseled	518
Total number vocational conferences held	711
Number of brief contacts with pupils	1.065
Number of group conferences with pupils	13
Trips made for pupils	14
Outside contacts regarding pupils	235
Hours of clerical work done by counselor	48
Addresses made	2
Meetings attended	15
Individual projects (hours)	45

Why occupational guidance is important in Cincinnati.— One of the important reasons for stressing educational and vocational counseling in the eighth and ninth grades in the schools of Cincinnati is the fact that pupils after completing the work of the eighth grade must choose between an academic education in an unspecialized high school and vocational training in some one of the 10 vocational high schools conducted under the Smith-Hughes act for vocational education. Transfer to a vocational high school may also be made by pupils who have entered a senior high school. It is therefore important that pupils at transition points in the school system be fully aware of the opportunities provided in the city for various types of training and that they receive counsel in making educational choices which will lead to the type of work in line with their interests and abilities.

There are no special counselors in the vocational high schools, and any counseling done in these schools is carried on by principals, coordinators, and teachers. It is assumed that a pupil on entering a vocational high school has made an occupational choice and is ready to prepare for a special vocation. Educational and vocational guidance, therefore, is emphasized prior to the time that the pupil elects a vocational high school. If his choice of a vocational high school proves to be unwise, he is helped to transfer to another school in which it is believed he will become adjusted more satisfactorily.

Cost of guidance and the services provided.—The cost of the Division of Occupational Research and Counseling in 1931–32 was approximately $21,000. The service provided by this amount reached 3,679 individual pupils with intensive personal conferences. There were provided 7,479 brief personal contacts with counselors for pupils who may have sought the advice of the counselor voluntarily or at the request of a teacher, principal, or parent. In addition, all pupils above the sixth grade (20,765) benefited indirectly from the work of the division through its research activities and publications.

The Life Advisement Bureau.—Guidance as a specific function of the secondary school was introduced in the public-school system of Milwaukee, Wis., in 1928, through the establishment of the Life Advisement Bureau. A director was appointed to consult with the principals of the high schools regarding the establishment of guidance services in the schools and to develop an organization designed to aid pupils in making school adjustments and in planning their life careers. In order to avoid a topheavy central organization, the personnel of the Life Advisement Bureau was restricted to the director, but any principal was permitted to assign any number of his teachers to guidance duties for such portion of their time as he might see fit to utilize, provided that the minimum teacher-pupil ratio of the school was not changed. The plan made possible the establishment of guidance services in every secondary school in the city through the cooperative planning of the director of life advisement and principals of the schools.

Development of guidance programs in individual schools.— In the beginning the personal activities of the director of the bureau were confined chiefly to the senior classes in the different schools. Definite assistance was offered in the choice of colleges and in the selection of life pursuits. In this work the director had the cooperation of most of the principals and the advisers of the senior classes. It was hoped that the influences of these activities would filter downward into the other classes of the secondary school. The consideration of the problems of twelfth-grade pupils revealed the necessity for anticipating and preventing the problems; hence, the emphasis was shifted to the freshman class. Teachers designated for advisory service in the different schools were at first asked to assume advisement duties in addition to their regular teaching assignments. As evidences of results were manifested in the schools releases

[84]

from teaching duties were granted by the principals to the advisers in proportion to the time needed for advisement service.

Evolving an organization for advisement services in the individual schools.—As the director of life advisement and the principals recognized special aptitude for counseling and guidance in the teachers who undertook the advisement services, chief advisers were designated to assume responsibilities for directing the work in the different schools. Assistants were then selected by the principal and chief adviser and assigned to special groups of pupils usually

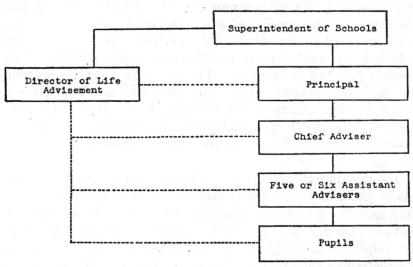

FIGURE 14.—Typical plan of organization for life-advisement service in secondary schools in Milwaukee. (Solid lines indicate executive responsibility; broken lines, consultative relationship)

without release from teaching duties or at most only partial release. Through direct supervision by the director of life advisement the advisers were gradually trained for guidance work and organizations were perfected by the principals which have made possible the development of a guidance program for all the pupils in the secondary schools. Figure 14 presents an organization which is considered typical of the organizations developed in the different schools, although variation from the type is by no means discouraged.

How the life-advisement organization functions in an individual secondary school.—In some of the schools the chief adviser devotes full time to guidance work, usually concentrating on the freshman class. These pupils are interviewed prior to admission, records are secured, tests are administered, courses are planned, parents are advised, schedules are made out, adjustments are effected, and individual advisement is provided. The assistant advisers are assigned to advanced groups, for which they are usually responsible during the residence of the group in the individual school. The work of the assistants is unified through the chief counselor, principal, and director of life advisement. All teachers engaged in advisement work are under the direction and supervision of the officers named. If aptitude, interest, and devotion to the work are not developed by the assistant advisers during the period of overtime service, they are relieved of guidance responsibilities before release from teaching duties is granted. The assistant advisers, as well as the chief adviser, must thus establish for themselves a place in the guidance organization of a given secondary school through an interneship of overtime advisory service before recognition is given in the form of release from teaching duties.

In the individual schools the advisers cooperate with classroom and home-room teachers, sponsors of extracurriculum activities, and administrative officers in the administration of pupils. Records are assembled in cumulative folders for pupils as individuals, diagnostic study is carried on, and corrective or remedial treatment is advised. In case pupils are required to seek employment, assistance is given in securing placement, and transfer to the part-time vocational school is arranged, if the individual is under 18 years of age. In the senior year guidance is provided for pupils in the choice of college or in the selection of a life work. Throughout the secondary-school period the primary concern of the adviser is individual adjustment to the opportunities provided by the school and life advisement for those who manifest an interest in choosing a vocation or are compelled by circumstances to enter upon a life career.

General advisement practices encouraged in all secondary schools.—The term "life advisement" as used in Milwaukee has a broader meaning than educational or vocational guidance considered separately. It encourages the study of the present performance of the individual pupil in the light of his tentative goals and future plans, as a means of inducing self-appraisal and self-discovery. To accomplish this purpose, certain general practices are encouraged by the director of advisement on the part of all the schools. As indicated in the following sections, these are (1) preadmission advisement, (2) follow-up of pupils after admission, (3) individual counseling, (4) group advisement, and (5) occupational information.

Preadmission advisement.—Since the greatest failure and loss from withdrawal occurs in the first year of the high-school course, the advisement service should undertake to overcome the break between the elementary or junior high school and the 4-year or senior high school. It is believed that much can be accomplished by all receiving schools through preadmission advisement of the following types:

(1) By giving the eighth-grade and ninth-grade graduates information regarding their new schools, curriculums, and subjects of study.

(2) By having the pupils meet and talk with their principal and (or) adviser from the high school to establish friendly confidence.

(3) By considering each graduate's individual needs, plans, interests, prospects, and abilities and helping him to select a program of studies for the high school in conjunction with his parents, grade principal, and eighth-grade teacher, using as a basis for advice a personnel record sheet showing his progress from first grade on, his scholastic record in the eighth grade, his mental age and educational age determined by tests given during the semester, together with an indication of his cooperation, behavior, effort, dependability, certain personality ratings as judged by his eighth-grade teacher, and a record of his outside interests and experiences.

(4) By enabling pupils to visit the school which they plan to enter and, where possible, to visit some of the classes which they will attend the following semester.

Follow-up of pupils after admission.—Every pupil who enters the school, whether by promotion or transfer, should have an interview and be followed up until completely adjusted. In an effort to facilitate success among incoming pupils the high schools should organize a careful assimilation or orientation program. These programs are usually worked out by the teacher committees under the general direction of the principal and immediate supervision of the adviser. Such adviser-teachers prepare an outline of guidance topics to be taken up at group meetings which occur briefly at regular intervals. Some of the topics considered are the school, its traditions, ideals, etc.; rules and regulations of the school; forming good study habits; study planning and study budgets; membership in school organizations; marks, their purpose and value; problems of conduct, etc.

Intensive individual work should also be carried on with first-semester pupils by the advisers. All freshmen should be given at least one interview to discover whether they are making the proper adjustments to school and classes and also to make them feel at home.

After the first reports are issued, those who receive unusually high marks should be sent for and commended for their diligence. The records of all freshmen should be scanned carefully and sympathetically, the object being to help the pupil to work up to the level of his ability. Follow-up work of a more intensive nature should be done with pupils who do not make the proper progress. Every time a pupil receives a failure mark on his report card he should be given a progress sheet containing the subject, teacher, mark, and the reason for the failure. Each week the pupil should be required to obtain a report to date from his teachers, which he in turn discusses with his adviser. This procedure should be carried on until the pupil secures a passing mark.

Individual counseling.—Individual counseling by advisers is encouraged by the Life Advisement Bureau. Pupils are invited to seek interviews with their advisers and the advisers are urged to confer with pupils who are reported as maladjusted in their work and who need counsel in the selection of courses, the choice of extracurriculum activities, and the planning of personal affairs.

In case a pupil proposes to leave the full-time school, investigation should be made, conference held, and an attempt made to persuade the pupil to remain in school if such action seems best. Assistance to the pupil is conditioned largely by the individual's remaining in school. If the investigation discloses necessity for leaving school, plans for the next step should be developed and provisions made for conference in case advice is desired by the pupil or reports of progress in employment by the adviser.

Individual conferences are advised in the case of seniors with regard to the choice of a college or the selection of an occupation. As a basis of such conferences the results of scholastic-aptitude tests, rank in class, and the ratings by the teachers of the personal traits and characteristics of the pupils are recommended for the use of the advisers instead of mere personal opinions.

Group advisement.—Group advisement is regarded as an economical method of dealing with the common needs of pupils, but it is not considered a substitute for individual counseling. The advisers through individual contacts will accumulate lists of problems which can be considered with groups. As a result, group conferences may be scheduled when in the judgment of the advisers such conferences are practicable.

Occupational information.—The lack of information among young people regarding vocations and vocational opportunities makes necessary a systematic attempt on the part of the school to compensate for the deficiency. This condition is met in part by some of the schools as follows: Monthly themes in English classes are prepared on topics listed for each grade and semester throughout the four years. These themes tend to stress the importance of "looking ahead," of "planning" instead of "drifting," and the necessity of "getting the facts" before choosing a course of action. A unit in ninth-grade community civics supplies a bird's-eye view of the world of work, develops the interrelation of various occupations, and presents a technique for investigating and judging an occupation. Detailed information is given by the teachers in all regular classrooms and in special subjects as interests in various careers emerge from the topics being studied. Teachers are expected to bring out the relationship and employ the technique for discussing the type of work mentioned. Life-work conferences are conducted on a regular schedule throughout the year by competent business and professional men and women. Industrial visits are made where they seem desirable and conferences held with the adviser or with one of the professional representatives. Other devices which have been found useful in extending the influence of life-advisement work are: Assembly programs, plays and concerts, school clubs, the school paper, the school handbook, motion pictures, the student council, the library, and "open house."

Features of life-advisement service in individual schools.—The director of life advisement has refused to impose a fixed program on the individual schools. He has chosen to accept the rôle of the consultant rather than of the executive. As a result the programs of life advisement in the different schools vary in many respects. Initiative on the part of the principals and advisers has been encouraged in the formulation of programs and in the development of specific guidance activities. Time did not permit visits to all the secondary schools in the city to observe features of programs which are considered characteristic of individual schools. Hence, only a few features are reported to illustrate the policy of the director in encouraging initiative on the part of principals and advisers in the different schools. These are presented in the three sections next following.

Advisement in connection with homogeneous grouping in the Riverside High School.—The Riverside High School has sought to adjust its curriculum and methods of teaching to the needs of pupils through the careful grouping of pupils in all of the grades. Tests are administered to pupils prior to admission in the ninth grade, elementary-school records are studied, parents are informed regarding the offerings of the school, and schedules are arranged to permit pupils to receive instruction in groups in which the materials and methods are planned with respect to the general level of ability of the group.

The chief adviser gives full time to the study and advisement of the first three half grades (9B, 9A, and 10B). Careful classification of pupils in the first year and a half of their residence in school on the basis of ability and accomplishment makes subsequent classification easier and averts much maladjustment and failure. Assistant advisers carry on the advisement work in the other grades, retaining their respective groups until the individuals graduate. The assistants are released from one teaching period daily for advisement duties, which consist in seeing pupils in need of attention at each 5-week working period and in giving daily service to pupils reported by teachers or seeking advisement on their own initiative.

The program of homogeneous grouping coupled with the advisement service has made possible the efficient administration of a pupil personnel of extreme social and economic differences in the Riverside High School. Grouping has not been stigmatized as has been reported in other schools, but it has served to make pupils happy in their work because of the grading of the materials of instruction and the adjustment of the methods of teaching to the needs of the respective groups. The fact that this plan is employed in all grades of this school has contributed to its success and has tended to eliminate the objections which are often raised against its use with the entering class only.

The home-room adviser in the Peckham Junior High School.—Life advisement in the Peckham Junior High School is carried on with 1,240 pupils by 1 part-time chief adviser, 6 class advisers, and 32 home-room advisers. The responsibilities and functions of the home-room advisers as defined by the principal and chief adviser of the school are:

(1) Orientation of the pupils.

(2) Maintenance of pupil morale.

(3) Development in the pupils of a wholesome attitude toward the school as a civic enterprise.

(4) Keeping carefully all necessary and required records of the pupils.

(5) Giving advice with respect to curriculum and other social activities.

(6) Acting as intermediary for the pupils with administrative and guidance officers, with teachers, and with parents.

(7) Keeping adequate personnel records of all the pupils.

(8) Individual counseling, both educational and vocational.

(9) Taking a friendly interest in each pupil and making the school a home for the pupil rather than a factory.

(10) By example and otherwise leading, guiding, and inspiring the pupils ethically, socially, and educationally with enthusiasm, sympathy, and fairness.

(11) Full cooperation with subject teachers and all administrative and guidance agencies in the school.

Each home-room adviser has a group of approximately 40 pupils for 15 minutes daily for 3 days of the week and for a 30-minute period once each week. A cumulative folder for each pupil of the group is kept by each adviser, and materials and records are filed for use in individual and group conferences. Since the home-room advisers also serve as teachers, it is possible through the careful differentiation of duties to secure a constructive coordination of effort in the advisement service. The advisement duties of teachers in the Peckham Junior High School are as follows:

(1) Maintain constantly a kindly interest in the welfare of each pupil.

(2) Sense the symptoms of maladjustment in a pupil in the incipient stages.

(3) Bring the guidance organization to bear on cases that need attention.

(4) Contribute to the diagnosis of the causes of maladjustment.

(5) Assist in the application of corrective or remedial measures advised.

(6) Give specific guidance to pupils in the pursuit of intellectual interests.

(7) Develop proper study habits.

(8) Develop proper conception of the processes of education and the opportunities for education provided through the school.

(9) Arouse interests related to his subject.

(10) Stress occupational implications of the subject.

(11) Meet individual needs and difficulties.

(12) Cooperate fully with every other teacher and all the guidance agencies in the school.

Development of potential leaders in the North Division High School.—A unique plan of guiding potential leaders in the development of leadership qualities is employed in the North Division High School. Two organizations, designated as the Boys' and Girls' Leadership Clubs, with a membership of 30 pupils in each club, each semester are sponsored by the advisers for the purpose of training pupils for the assumption of responsibilities in positions in the school requiring pupil leadership.

The membership of the clubs is derived from two sources: (1) Pupils who have been designated by members of the faculty as possessing potential qualities of leadership, and (2) pupils holding positions of leadership in the school who feel the need of advisement in carrying on the duties of their offices. The clubs meet weekly at the fifth period of the school day with their sponsors. The members eat their lunches together and then spend about a half hour in discussing problems and qualities of leadership.

The clubs are in no sense honorary organizations. Their primary function is the guidance of pupils above the freshman level in the study of leadership responsibilities and the qualities of successful leaders. The sponsors of the clubs, through the stimulation of formal and informal discussion on the part of the members, seek to provide a type of guidance for potential leaders which will result in the undertaking of leadership problems and the awakening of a desire to serve the school through the use of qualities possessed.

Cost of life-advisement service.—Except for the salary of the director of life advisement and a few hundred dollars for tests, supplies, pamphlets, and books, the life-advisement program has not cost the school system of Milwaukee anything beyond what would have been spent anyway. The full-time and part-time advisers were relieved from classroom teaching by principals who considered the advisement service of sufficient value to warrant reorganization of the schedule. The ratio of teachers to pupils in the secondary schools has not been changed and no additional teachers have been employed to carry the teaching duties formerly assumed by the advisers. If the total cost of the advisement service were charged to the secondary schools—which would be unfair, because the director also serves the elementary schools—it would amount to approximately 20 cents per pupil.

Results claimed for life advisement.—The results claimed in part for the program of life advisement in the 11 high schools of Milwaukee are reduction in the rate of failure, reduction in withdrawals from school, and economy in the per credit cost of instruction. Comparison of data with respect to the foregoing claims for the years covered by the advisement program shows a gradual realization of the results sought. Considering all subjects in the high schools for the first semester of the year 1928–29, when life advisement was introduced, the median rate of pupil failures in the 11 schools was 16.9 per cent. For the first semester of 1931–32 the median was 12.3 per cent, or a reduction of 4.6 per cent. In the ninth grade the median rate of failure for the same semesters was reduced from 19.1 to 14.4 per cent.

Between 1928 and 1931 the percentage of pupils withdrawing from the regular high schools decreased from 12.9 per cent to 9.2, and in the technical high schools from 23 per cent to 14.3. These results are not claimed for the life-advisement service alone, since other improvements in the work of the school may have influenced some of the pupils to remain longer in school. Besides, schools everywhere have tended in recent years to retain pupils through more school years. However, since the advisers sought specifically to prevent withdrawals through adjustment and life advisement, it is fair to assume that the positive character of the results are in part accounted for by the advisement service.

Data on the cost of instruction in the high schools show that the per credit costs were decreased from $14.88 to $12.57 between 1928 and 1931, a fact attributed by the principals very largely to the introduction of the advisement service. It is, of course, impossible to separate the influence of the advisers from the effects of possible improvements in instruction, supervision, and administration in the reduction of credit costs through the prevention of failure and withdrawal. Since the pupils and the schools have benefited from the service to a degree not evidenced before the introduction of the life-advisement program, it is reasonable to assume that the general influence has been positive and, in so far as many individuals are concerned, especially helpful.

CHAPTER IX : CASE REPORT ON THE MILWAUKEE VOCATIONAL SCHOOL

Legal basis of part-time education.—By legislative action in 1911 the State of Wisconsin provided that communities of more than 5,000 population must maintain a local board of industrial education for the purpose of fostering, establishing, and maintaining industrial, commercial, continuation, and evening schools and that communities of less than 5,000 population may have such a board. The law requires that children between 14 and 16 years of age engaged in remunerative work must attend school four hours a week. Subsequent amendments to the law have increased the age period of continuation education to between 14 and 18 years and compulsory attendance to eight hours per week.

The Milwaukee Vocational School is a development of the Wisconsin law of 1911. It is independent of the public-school system of Milwaukee in its organization and administration, although it functions in close articulation with the public schools in receiving or returning by transfer pupils whose educational status is determined by the necessity of remunerative work.

The work of the vocational school.—The vocational school is concerned chiefly with employed pupils over 14 years of age who have completed the work of the eight elementary grades. Pupils over 14 years of age who have spent nine years in school but have not completed the work of the eighth grade may be admitted to the vocational school. The school also accepts full-time pupils in all departments, and maintains two departments which serve full-time pupils only— the full-time commercial and the vocational departments.

Junior pupils attend school one-half of each day until the end of the quarter in which they become 16 years of age. Senior pupils attend school one full day a week until the end of the quarter in which they become 18. Evening-school attendants must be 16 years old or more.

The normal annual cumulative enrollment of the Milwaukee Vocational School is approximately 22,000, nearly two-thirds of the number being enrolled in the day school. The pupils served are those who desire to seek gainful employment during the secondary-school period (age 14 to 18) and to receive vocational as well as general secondary education.

The need of the pupils for guidance.—The immediate economic needs of the pupils attending the Milwaukee Vocational School, as well as the necessity for their occupational orientation, makes guidance on the part of the school imperative. The pupils need guidance in seeking employment; in self-appraisal and analysis of interest in try-out courses at the junior level; in the choice of an occupation at the senior level; in personal, social, and civic adjustments to the life of the school; in overcoming difficulties in classroom work and in employment; and in meeting home and community responsibilities. Accordingly, guidance is made a major departmental responsibility of the school comparable in importance with instruction and business administration and closely articulated with instruction and business administration. Through guidance the adjustment of the pupil to the opportunities of the school and to employment is effected.

Organization of the guidance department.—The guidance department of the Milwaukee Vocational School is the resultant of a series of developments. Prior to 1926 the chief function of guidance was placement, which was attended to by the several department heads of the school. In January, 1926, a placement secretary was appointed who made approximately 1,000 placements that year. In August, 1927, a placement department was established with an officer (man) at the head whose chief duty was field promotional work. Three months later a second officer (woman) was added to handle the placement of girls. Shortly after the second appointment an assistant was added to the department, which completed the staff for that year. In September, 1928, the staff was enlarged by the addition of a registrar, general stenographer, and clerical assistant, the assistant of the previous year being assigned to the field of domestic counseling.

The name of the department was officially designated "The Employment-Guidance Department" in December, 1928, at which time an experienced personnel man was added to take charge of miscellaneous mercantile counseling. By March of the following year an experienced counselor for pupils in the building trades was appointed, increasing the staff to six officers and two clerks. On account of a gradual shift in the emphasis of the duties of the department from placement to guidance, the name of the department was officially changed in September, 1929, to "Guidance-Employment Division," the present departmental designation. Since 1929 an office-trades counselor and another full-time clerk have been added, increasing the staff to eight officials and three clerks. The assignment of duties to the different members of the staff is on the functional basis, the member accepting responsibility for guidance, placement, and follow-up work in the occupations to which his training and experience warrant his assignment.

The head of the division is officially designated the director and the assistants as coordinators. The duties of a coordinator are usually restricted to one or more occupational fields. Pupils electing an occupation within the field of a given coordinator are referred on admission to the school to this coordinator for classification and assignment to classes and subsequent guidance unless the pupil transfers to some other occupational field.

The coordinators keep in touch with the industries of the city by making surveys of the opportunities for placement and collecting facts regarding occupational changes and developments. The findings of coordinators are referred to the research department of the instructional division, which investigates the developments and reports to the head of the instructional division the needs for modifications in courses and methods. The coordinator also looks after pupil placement in his respective occupational field and makes follow-up studies of pupils previously placed. Contacts with the instructors in the coordinator's field are direct, and every effort is made to articulate the work of the school with the employment of the pupils.

The organization of the Guidance-Employment Division as an integral part of the vocational school is shown in Figure 15.

Instructing the pupils regarding the guidance services of the school.—As a means of acquainting the pupils with the guidance service provided by the school, a special unit on the Guidance-Employment Division is provided for discussion in the classes of the general-subject teachers. The instruction sheet on the unit states the purposes of the division as (1)

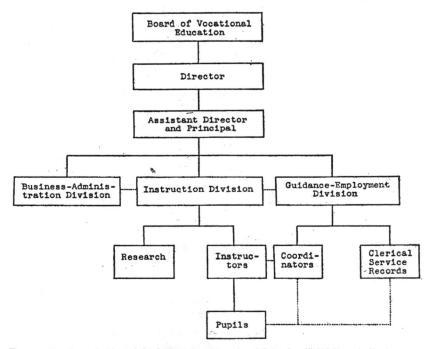

FIGURE 15.—Organization of the Milwaukee Vocational School. (Solid lines indicate executive responsibilities; broken lines, contact relations)

helping boys and girls choose the work for which they are best fitted and (2) placing boys and girls in positions in accordance with their occupational adaptabilities. The following instructions and questions are then given:

This unit is not going to be about the young fellow who went wrong because he had no trade or occupation and did not turn out to be a respected self-supporting citizen. Rather, we want to help you to "find yourself," so that in a few years you will be able to support yourself and provide for a home. Oh! don't laugh. Figures for our State prove that the marriageable age is between 20 and 24 for men and the same for women. How many more years have you to think things over, to choose, and to learn some definite trade or occupation?

The Employment-Guidance Division is in a position to know the employment situation in the city and to advise students with reference to the trade or occupation to enter. The requirements of different trades and occupations vary and must be met by the applicant. Educational requirements are growing higher and higher, and some employers will not consider an applicant unless he is a high-school graduate. No matter what our viewpoint might be on this matter, the man who pays the wages or salary is the one who sets certain standards for his employees.

Now let us ask ourselves three questions:
1. Who can use the Employment and Guidance Department?
2. When should one use the department?
3. How can one best use the department?

Consider each one of these questions and see what it means. Take question No. 1. *Who can use the department?*

This division of the school is open to the youth of the city, but it is especially operated for the students of the school, including night-school students. The majority of calls from employers ask for boys and girls ranging in age from 14 to 18. Some older people also ask for help. Parents are especially invited for consultation. Appointments should be made by the students for their parents.

When should one use the Guidance-Employment Division?

Some students are of the opinion that they must be out of work before leaving an application for employment. This is not true. Any student who wishes to leave an application may do so. He may be working and dissatisfied, or he may be unemployed. In either case an application should be filled out and taken personally to the employment division. When you are out of work or want to change, let your shop teacher or home-room teacher know about it. Blank applications are kept by all home or shop teachers and can be had for the asking. These should be filled out by the applicant. Write in ink as neatly as possible and answer all questions. Your teacher will check your application and give you your rating on the back of the card.

Just a word should be added about this rating given you by your shop teacher. It is to your advantage if this rating is "good" or better. Frequently employers call up and want a boy or girl who has certain qualities. We must match these qualities as nearly as we can. The rating on the back of each application tells the story. A boy in plumbing can hardly expect to be placed in a bakery or a boy in woodwork in a job in barbering. Yet some students wonder why they are never placed in certain kinds of work for which they are asking on their applications. Your first choice of work desired should be something like the shop subject taken here. Try to "find" yourself as soon as possible, so you may learn just as much as you can before you are 18

[99]

years of age. Too many students come to the Employment-Guidance Division with no choice of work. When asked what their first choice would be, they answer, "Anything." Did you ever go into a grocery store and, when asked what you wished, answer, "Anything"? Remember there are many occupations, thousands of them, and so you must state at least your first and second choices.

How can one best use the department?

First of all, the student should have a conference with his shop teacher. After you have been in a shop a few weeks, your instructor will be able to judge you pretty well and be able to advise you concerning your capabilities as a workman in that particular trade. Our experience has been that the estimates of your shop teacher and your employer have been, as a rule, the same.

If you have any doubt in your mind after this talk, why not have an interview with some one in the Employment and Guidance Division?

Still another step can be taken, and perhaps it is a better one. Talk things over with your parents and, if possible, arrange with some one in the Employment and Guidance Division to talk with you and your parents some evening.

Your likes and dislikes are very important. Let us know about them. Feel free to talk when you come in. Our talks will be strictly confidential.

The following problems for study and discussion are listed:

1. Where do you get the application blanks?
2. Who should fill out the application?
3. When should you come to the Employment and Guidance Department?
4. How can the Employment and Guidance Department be of service to you besides getting you a job?
5. What is the best way for a student in the Milwaukee Vocational School to prepare for his life work?
6. What are some of the desirable qualities that students should develop to insure success?
7. How may the teacher's estimate help you to secure a job?
8. A written report on the general class discussion is also required.

Indirect guidance.—Films are shown daily at the noon assembly period for the information and enjoyment of the pupils and with the idea of providing incidental guidance. Some of the films are prepared by the guidance department and deal with subjects like "How to Apply for a Job." The bulletin board of the school is also used to attract the attention of the pupils to important matters, usually presented in well-planned posters. The guidance department also utilizes the biweekly newspaper of the school to present to the pupils regularly important aspects of the guidance service. The following article, which explains the purpose of the follow-up slip, is illustrative of the use made of the newspaper by the Guidance-Employment Division:

The follow-up slips.—Have you ever wondered what was the significance of the little white slip which called you to the Guidance-Employment Division? That little slip is called the "follow-up slip" and it serves a multitude of purposes.

When the employment department places its boys and girls on jobs, its work is not finished; in fact, it has only begun! We are interested in knowing what happens after you are on the job, and we do this in two ways. One is the employer follow-up; the other, the employee follow-up.

In order to make the employer follow-up, one of the counselors goes into the factory, store, or office where you may be working and talks with your supervisor. He is interested in your progress, your hours and wages, and your chances for promotion. In the employee follow-up we call you in to see us. During this interview we get your reaction to your job. We want you to be perfectly frank with us, for we assure you that all information you give us is strictly confidential.

With all this extra work, it certainly is necessary to show great results. And there are great results from follow-up. Oftentimes there are conditions of work which are corrected. Many times the employer has some small grievance which can be smoothed out. Very often job adjustments are effected.

So when you receive the little white slip from room 222, remember that the idea that we want to help you has prompted the sending of it to you. When you report, let us know exactly how you are getting along. Remember, our interest in you does not stop when you have been placed on the job, but increases the longer you are there.

Try-out courses.—Nine general try-out courses for junior boys between 14 and 16 years of age are offered in building trades, metal trades, auto trades, printing trades, electrical trades, woodworking trades, business practice, and graphic arts. Each of these courses may be pursued for a period of 10 weeks with the idea of discovering interests and aptitudes. Similar courses for girls are offered in trades providing employment opportunities for girls. The pupils divide their time equally between the trade teachers and the teachers of general subjects. At 16 a pupil is eligible to enter apprenticeship training. The try-out courses are intended to assist pupils in finding a trade in case apprenticeship training is desired.

Pupils who enter the vocational school after the sixteenth birthday omit the try-out courses and elect an occupation on the advice of a coordinator from the group of 50 occupational courses offered. The teacher of the occupational course elected by the pupil cooperates with the coordinator in the adjustment of the pupil to his chosen occupation or in finding an occupation in which the individual is better fitted to succeed.

Procedure in securing assistance from the Guidance-Employment Division.—All applications of pupils for employment are made through their vocational teachers. An application form is filled out by the pupil with the advice of the teacher. First choice of position is for life's vocation, and second choice is for temporary employment. The pupil is then sent with the card to the Guidance-Employment Division for personal interview. The application is filed according to the kind of job requested and receives attention in response to employers' requests. A special effort is made by the division for pupils highly recommended by their teachers. The application is also used in the placement of apprentices.

Placement service.—The number of placements for any given year will necessarily vary with the conditions which determine placements. For 1930, 3,606 pupils secured placements through recommendations of the division. This service is essential to the vocational school and is one of the important reasons for the existence of the Guidance-Employment Division. The aim of the division is not merely to aid the pupil in getting a job but in securing the right kind of job when possible through which the individual's relations between school and employment may be carried on most profitably.

Follow-up service.—The follow-up service of the Guidance-Employment Division consists very largely in industrial contacts designed to facilitate employment and to serve as mediator between employer and employee in promoting satisfactory relations. The extent of this service is indicated by the fact that the officers of the department make on the average approximately 2,000 calls on employers during the school year.

The aims of the Guidance-Employment Division.—The aims of the Guidance-Employment Division of the Milwaukee Vocational School, stated in terms of the services which it undertakes to render to pupils, are:

(1) To have the individual consider every phase of the problem before leaving the full-time school.

(2) To assist the individual in entering the trade-finding course which will enable him better to choose his life work.

(3) To give the individual reliable information concerning job opportunities.

(4) To establish a central place to which all calls for young people will come and to which all young people will apply for work.

(5) To help the individual master the proper manner in applying for and holding a job.

(6) To assist the individual in securing the right job.

(7) To make more rapid advancement possible by contacting the individual's employer.

(8) To discuss with the individual's parents any questions pertaining to his school work or job which they may care to bring to the department.

(9) To make the proper follow-ups after the individual has been placed on a job, both with the individual and with his employer, to see that he is progressing, and to make any adjustment needed.

(10) To make the individual feel welcome at all times.

Cost of the guidance and employment service.—The annual cost of the guidance and employment service in the Milwaukee Vocational School is approximately $1 per pupil enrolled. If only the employment service is considered, the cost is approximately $6 per individual placed. However, the scope of the work of the department for the pupils is much broader than placement and must be evaluated in terms of the numerous services rendered, ranging from incidental guidance to individual diagnosis, remedial treatment, and placement.

CHAPTER X : CASE REPORT ON THE JOLIET TOWNSHIP
HIGH SCHOOL

The personnel department.—The personnel department of
the Joliet Township High School and Junior College was
established in 1912 for the purpose of guiding pupils in the
choice of curriculums and in their subsequent progress
through school. The authors of the plan wisely separated
the functions of administration and guidance, placing the
former under administrative officers and home-room teachers
and the latter under an advisory committee of teachers. In
1922 a personnel director was added to the school staff to
articulate and direct the work of the committee advisers and
to serve as the head of the guidance work in the school. At
that time an elaborate record system was introduced which
has since been simplified. The functions of the personnel
department are now educational and vocational guidance,
recommendation and placement, testing, recording, and
research.

Organization of the personnel department.—The organization of the personnel department is shown in Figure 16.
The director is an executive officer with respect to guidance
functions and a consulting officer with respect to other
functions. This form of organization fixes responsibility on
the personnel department for pupil guidance and avoids
the complications which may arise in the administration of
other functions. For example, the making of a pupil's schedule of classes is the responsibility of the committee adviser
to whom the pupil is assigned, and change in the schedule
can be made only by this committeeman. Complaint may
be made to the committee adviser by a classroom or home-
room teacher regarding the schedule of a pupil, but the responsibility for the adjustment rests with the committeeman,
who may secure the advice of the personnel director if it is
needed.

Need for personnel service in Joliet Township High School and Junior College.—The need for personnel service by the pupils of this school is acute. The pupils are drawn from 25 different nationalities, 77 per cent of the parents being foreign born. The pupils come from four sources—eighth-grade graduates of the public elementary schools of Joliet, graduates of parochial schools of different religious-nationality groups, graduates of the eighth grade in rural schools in non-high-school districts, and transfer pupils from other high schools who have moved to Joliet. The annual enrollment of the school is approximately 3,500. The withdrawals

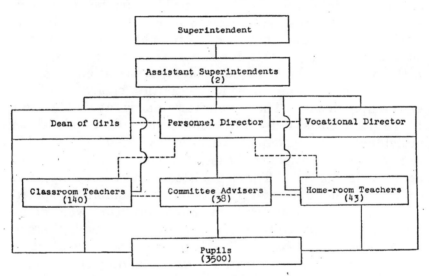

FIGURE 16.—Organization of the personnel department of the Joliet Township High School and Junior College. (Solid lines indicate executive responsibility; broken lines, contact relationships)

average about 7 per cent annually, and the failures approximate 8 per cent. The responsibility for adjusting this heterogeneous group of pupils to the 30 curriculums of the school rests with the personnel department.

Preadmission guidance.—One month prior to graduation from the city elementary schools and rural schools the pupils are addressed by one of the administrative officers of the secondary school. At this time elective cards and the handbook are distributed. About two weeks later members of the advisory committee visit the schools, conferring with the pupils and giving advice in the choice of curriculums. The elective card previously distributed is signed by pupil and parent and is made the basis of the schedule of classes for the entering class of the ensuing semester. If a mistake is made in the choice of a curriculum, the error may be rectified by the advising committeeman on the opening day of school when the pupil presents himself for admission. The success of preadmission curriculum guidance is attested by the fact that seldom do the changes in elections by a given class amount to more than 2 per cent of the choices made.

The work of the individual committee advisers.—An individual committeeman usually is assigned 100 freshmen on their admittance to the secondary school. These pupils are retained during their membership in school, the committee adviser being responsible for the advisement of the pupils with respect to choice of curriculum, registration, progress in classes, membership in school activities, choice of college, and employment. The committeeman is available from 11 to 12 o'clock daily for conference with pupils either individually or in groups. This service is rendered in addition to regular teaching duties, but compensation of $100 per year is allowed. The committee adviser not only gives counsel to the pupils and parents but is available for conference with classroom or home-room teachers who desire information or advice regarding the committeeman's charges.

The home-room teacher.—The home-room teacher is not an adviser but an administrative officer, having charge of a group of pupils one period daily for purpose of record and supervised study. Pupils may be excused by the home-room teacher for library reading, conference with committee advisers, or participation in school activities of semicurriculum character, such as band, orchestra, and glee club.

Occupational information.—A half-year course in occupations is provided for freshmen. The purpose of the course is to aid the pupils in school orientation; in acquiring an extensive knowledge of occupations through reading, class discussion, industrial visitation, and talks by representatives of occupations; and in the intensive examination of a favored occupation through the preparation of a career book. The course is taught by a member of the social-science department who has made special preparation for the work required. Libraries on occupations are provided for all classrooms in which the course on occupations is taught.

General exploratory courses.—All freshmen are required to take a year of general science, which is organized as an exploratory course, and a year of general shop or general home economics. The general shop course consists of six 6-week units in six different shops and the general home economics course of three 12-week units in the three aspects of home economics, namely, cooking, sewing, and home care. Exploratory courses in music and art are also provided for both first-year and second-year pupils. The aim of the school is to bring to bear on the pupil its entire resources, to the end that self-discovery may be an outcome of the freshman year.

Teacher reports to committee advisers.—At intervals of six weeks throughout the school year the classroom teachers report to the committee advisers on the progress of pupils. The marks are recorded on the record cards of the pupils by the several committee advisers, and conferences are held with individual pupils when considered desirable. The semester marks are transcribed from the committee record cards to the cumulative record cards of the pupil twice each year by secretaries in the central office. The record card is the property of the committee adviser, except that it must be kept on file in the central office. All recording is a matter of clerical routine, except the reports of the classroom teachers to the committee advisers and the transfer of the pupils' periodic marks by the committeemen to the individual record cards.

Cumulative record folders.—Certain personnel records are accumulated in pocket-file folders in the central office, consisting of the ratings of teachers on personal traits and abilities, letters written and received regarding the pupils, misconduct reports, information reports on participation in activities collected from pupils by home-room teachers near the close of the year, the admission blank of the pupil containing photograph, the scores made on standardized tests, and the annual scholastic record cards of the committee advisers. The records of each pupil for each year are stapled together and filed in the cumulative folder, in order that they may be available for study when data other than the scholastic marks on the cumulative record card of a pupil are desired for purposes of guidance or recommendation.

Annual rating of personal traits and abilities.—Each classroom teacher is expected to rate each pupil semiannually on the development of personal traits and abilities. The form used is as shown in Figure 17. This form is stapled in the cumulative folder each semester as a progressive record of the character development of the pupil during his residence in the school. It is used chiefly by classroom teachers and committee advisers in the diagnostic study of pupils.

INDIVIDUAL RATING RECORD

Name of student _

Quality	Rating
I. Sustained application _ _ _ _ _ _ _ _ _ _ _ _ _ _ _	1 2 3 4 5
II. Ability to organize_ _ _ _ _ _ _ _ _ _ _ _ _ _ _ _	1 2 3 4 5
III. Promptness _	1 2 3 4 5
IV. Accuracy_ _	1 2 3 4 5
V. Leadership ability_ _ _ _ _ _ _ _ _ _ _ _ _ _ _ _	1 2 3 4 5
VI. Social qualities _ _ _ _ _ _ _ _ _ _ _ _ _ _ _ _ _	1 2 3 4 5

Subject: _

Remarks: _

_ _

Signature of Rater.

FIGURE 17.—Form used by teachers in the Joliet Township High School and Junior College in rating the personal traits and abilities of pupils

Indirect guidance through the handbook.—A handbook is published each year as a school project under the sponsorship of the student council for the general information of incoming pupils who are unfamiliar with the opportunities, practices, and traditions of the school. It contains brief instructions to pupils and an account of the school rules, regulations, and activities. The purpose of the publication is the guidance of the new pupil in the development of a spirit of cooperation through the information presented in the book.

Extramural guidance services.—A number of influences having bearing on guidance are carried on without the regular activities and personnel of the school. One hundred members of the Kiwanis Club contribute their services through the personnel director to boys who desire to confer with representative men in the community regarding occupational problems. Medical examination for girls is secured through the service of a woman physician who is a member of the board of education. A similar service for boys is secured from practicing physicians of the city.

Activities of the personnel director.—The personnel director is the head of the personnel department. He administers the standardized tests required by the superintendent, arranges for scoring these tests, and reports the results to the faculty of the school. He sets up the procedure for filing data in the cumulative folders of the pupils and organizes the data for use in the selection of pupils for honors, in recommending graduates and former pupils to colleges and to employers. In order that the director may cooperate most effectively with the committee of advisers, he serves as a committeeman for a small group of pupils and is a member of the advisory committees for the different high-school grades. He is available for personal conferences with individual pupils who may desire his advice, especially members of the senior class desiring to have the greatest possible aid in the choice of a college.

Perhaps the most arduous duties of the personnel director are those pertaining to placement and research. Most of the placements (about 500 per year) are made through the director. It is his responsibility to make the contacts with employers, to confer with the committee advisers regarding the applications for placement, and to set in motion the procedures which result in the contact between the employer and the pupil seeking employment. Satisfactory service by the director depends on accuracy of records, knowledge of pupils, parents, employment conditions, and the collection and interpretation of data pertaining to the pupil personnel. In brief, the director of personnel is a student of the science of education, which is made possible through his systematic collection and organization of facts and his study of the problems affecting the pupil personnel of the school.

Cost of personnel service in the Joliet Township High School and Junior College.—The total cost of the personnel service in the Joliet Township High School and Junior College is approximately $2 per pupil each year. This includes three-fourths of the time of the personnel director, the services of 38 committee advisers at $100 each per year, and an estimated clerical service for transcribing records of $600 per year. The services rendered by this group of personnel officers, although considered important to the regular work of the school, should be charged to the guidance program.

Appraisal of the service of the personnel department.—Any appraisal of the service of the personnel department must rest on its value to the pupils of the school. This can be visualized only in terms of individual cases, which can be multiplied to provide a true picture of the worth of the department to the school. The following cases are typical of many which can be cited to illustrate the character of the service rendered by the personnel department to individual pupils.

CASE 1.—Howard Smith, a senior from the country, came to the personnel office last September for assistance in finding employment that would enable him to pay for his board and room. Within a week he was placed as elevator boy in an apartment hotel, working from 3.30 to 11.30 p. m. He was permitted to study in his cage and did satisfactory high-school work. During the second semester Howard worked 68 hours per week, earning 40 cents per hour. and carrying four subjects in school with an average grade of 80.

CASE 2.—John Moran's father was an electrical contractor. After the death of the father, John's mother secured work in a department store to support the family. In January the manager of the telephone company asked for a young man to take charge of the long-distance relays in the local telephone exchange. John, a senior in the 4-year industrial electrical course, was recommended, and after a careful investigation and try-out was given a job. The fact that he holds a Government broadcasting license for his amateur short-wave station was a material factor in securing him the position. He began work February 1 at $120 per month, working from 1 to 7 a. m., and attending high school for the forenoon session only. He continued his membership in the United States High School Championship Band and did satisfactory work in his studies. At present he has a permanent full-time position with the telephone company.

CASE 3.—Karl Graff, a senior of German parentage, was doing excellent work in the industrial print shop 4-year curriculum, where he also acted as linotype operator on the staff of the high-school paper. At the mid-year his parents moved to a city of 20,000 population in southern Wisconsin, where only academic courses were offered in the high school. Karl, who was anxious to complete his course in printing, applied to the personnel office for a job that would enable him to pay his expenses and remain in Joliet until the end of the school year. At the beginning of the second semester he was placed in the print shop of a local corporation, where he worked from 3.30 to 11.30 p. m., printing cartoons and advertising matter, at 40 cents per hour.

Despite this heavy schedule, he earned a place in the National Honor Society and was popular with his fellow pupils. After graduation, in June, 1928, he accepted a position as full-time linotype operator in the newspaper office of his home town in southern Wisconsin—a position which usually requires from two to four years of apprenticeship training.

CASE 4.—Mary Warren entered high school in September and enrolled in the secretarial-service curriculum. At the end of her first semester her name was on the "honor roll" with an average of 91. This and her high rank in the freshmen intelligence tests led her adviser to suggest that she consider with her parents the advisability of changing to a college-preparatory curriculum. Her parents were not sure that it would be possible for her to go to college, but readily consented to the change when the adviser showed how Mary could meet college-entrance requirements, and at the same time take much of the work necessary for secretarial service. A written request signed by her parents and countersigned by her committee adviser was filed in her personnel folder and she was transferred to the literature and arts "B" curriculum.

During her first summer vacation Mary worked for a month in her uncle's office, but did not like the work. Her next two summer vacations were spent in the summer session of the high school, where she earned enough credits to enable her to be graduated in three and one-half years.

At the end of her third year her committee adviser found that Mary had maintained an average of 92 since entering high school. As she was also given a high rating by her instructors in character, leadership, and service, the other three requisites, she was recommended for membership in the National High School Honor Society.

Because of her summer-school work Mary completed her high-school course in February of her senior year and, after consultation with the dean, decided to enter the Joilet Junior College at once. She was influenced in this decision by the fact that she was eligible for one of the scholarships available to worthy students of high standing and good reputation.

CHAPTER XI : CASE REPORT ON NEW TRIER TOWNSHIP HIGH SCHOOL

General organization of the plan.—The adviser-personnel plan of the New Trier Township High School has been established to provide educational, vocational, social, moral, and ethical guidance and counsel to all the pupils of the school. The staff organization consists of (1) the principal; (2) a dean of boys; (3) a dean of girls; (4) eight adviser chairmen (four men and four women); (5) a group of room advisers corresponding to home-room teachers; and (6) a director of research in charge of a department of reference, research, and placement. The organization is so planned that instructional, administrative, and disciplinary functions are integrated with the adviser-personnel organization.

The New Trier Township High School enrolls more than 2,000 pupils. The pupils are assigned to the room advisers on their entrance to high school and, with few exceptions, remain in the same group for the entire four years in school. There are 61 rooms in the advisory organization, 30 for the girls and 31 for the boys. The advisers function under the direction of adviser chairmen, the adviser chairmen under the dean of boys and dean of girls, and the deans under the principal.

The plan of organization as originally developed by the late superintendent of the school, Dr. F. E. Clerk, is shown in Figure 18. The routine channels of responsibility and authority in personnel and academic matters are shown by solid and broken lines. Two functions are expected of teachers, namely, advisory functions in the personnel field and instructional functions in the academic field. Although the functions are segregated in the diagram, the teacher may in many instances act both as an adviser and instructor of a pupil if the pupil happens to be a member of some class and of the adviser group of the teacher. In case of emergency matters, the channel of routine is indicated in the figure by the arrows.

Duties of the officers—(1) *The deans.*—The dean of boys and the dean of girls are the executive heads of the adviser-personnel system. They assign adviser chairmen to the

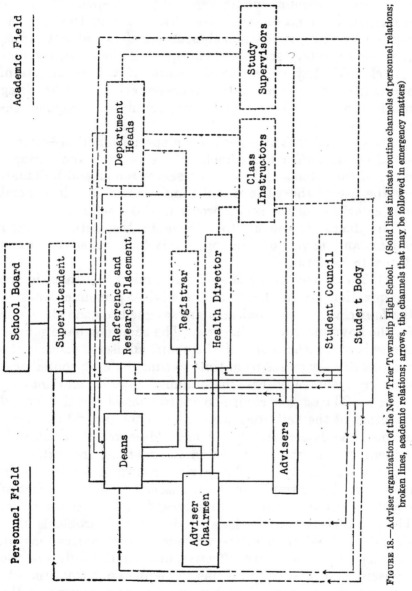

FIGURE 18.—Adviser organization of the New Trier Township High School. (Solid lines indicate routine channels of personnel relations; broken lines, academic relations; arrows, the channels that may be followed in emergency matters)

various classes and advisers to the adviser groups. They also make changes in the adviser groups, moving pupils from one group to another whenever necessary. The deans function as the disciplinary officers under the principal. They receive all cases of discipline from the adviser chairmen, advisers, or classroom teachers, and are the final authority in all cases, recommending expulsion or suspension to the principal when necessary. The deans, acting through the registrar's office, are responsible for transfers and certificates to other secondary schools or colleges. As heads of the personnel field they supervise the work of college selection, arranging for visits by college representatives and handling matters pertaining to scholarship, inquiries, recommendations, and awards.

The dean of girls also performs a special function—that of social chairman for the school. She supervises the arrangement of the calendar of events, reserves rooms and buildings for the use of the various clubs and classes, and in general acts as arbiter of the social program of the school.

The deans devote all their time to the duties of their offices, and have no teaching, study-hall, or adviser-room duties to perform.

(2) *The adviser chairmen.*—Eight adviser chairmen in the organization are in charge of the adviser-personnel work in the four classes; two chairmen are assigned to each class, one for the boys and one for the girls. The chairmen have general supervision of the work of the room advisers, visiting the various adviser rooms from time to time, holding conferences with the room advisers, maintaining records, and making reports. The adviser chairmen are responsible for the general direction of the activities carried on in the individual rooms during the adviser periods. A marked degree of variation is evident among the chairmen in the method and extent of supervising this work. The adviser chairman for the freshmen boys, for example, prepares a series of weekly bulletins which are sent to the room advisers under his direction. These bulletins contain lists of duties and problems that should be dealt with in the adviser period, suggestions on carrying out in the most effective manner the duties of the advisers, and reports and forms to be filled out from time to time for the purpose of making studies of the work of the advisers. This plan of weekly bulletins is not followed by any other chairman, although all give some form of super-

vision and help to the advisers in regard to the details of the program that is followed in the adviser period.

The adviser chairmen serve as the social chairmen for their classes. They sponsor all class activities, and their permission is secured before any class function is held. These officers consider cases of discipline referred to them by the advisers or by the classroom teachers and, if they can not adjust the problems satisfactorily, report the cases to the deans. The chairmen also are responsible for supervising the registration of the pupils in classes and for all adjustments of programs.

Several adviser chairmen have specific duties that apply to the entire student body, in addition to the duties directly related to their own classes. For example, the senior chairmen are responsible for considering college-entrance requirements. They check over and inspect the scholastic programs of all seniors from time to time to see that the entrance requirements for the colleges selected by the pupils are being met. They also arrange for representatives of various colleges to come to the high school for the purpose of acquainting the pupils with the colleges.

The chairman of the junior boys is responsible for the administrative duties connected with the assignment of lockers. The chairman of the sophomore boys is responsible for the supervision of automobiles used by the pupils. The chairman of the freshman boys also serves as registrar for the school. The other chairmen likewise have special duties that involve the entire student body in addition to supervising the work of the advisers in their own class groups.

(3) *The advisers.*—There are 61 advisers in the organization at present—9 for the freshman boys and 9 for the freshman girls, 8 for the sophomore boys and 8 for the sophomore girls, 8 for the junior boys and 7 for the girls, and 6 for the senior boys and 6 for the girls. Each of these advisers has about 35 pupils in his group, and usually is in charge of the same group for the entire period that the pupils remain in school.

The room advisers are responsible for administrative duties as well as duties directly related to the adviser-personnel program of the school. Matters of discipline are reported to the advisers by the classroom teachers. Frequently, however, these matters are reported directly to the adviser chairmen or to the deans, in which cases the room advisers are notified of the problems by the other officers. The advisers have no disciplinary powers or duties. In case the advisers become involved in problems of discipline, they act as counselors for the pupils in trouble. Because of this arrangement the room adviser is nearly always the officer in the adviser-personnel program to whom the pupils first turn when in need of counsel. The room advisers, consequently, are a selected group of teachers who have proved their interest in high-school pupils and their effectiveness in dealing with all types of problems that affect them.

The room advisers are responsible for a number of other administrative duties, such as (a) the inspection of the lockers of the pupils in their groups, (b) attendance reports, (c) details of registration, and (d) the reading of the official daily school bulletin of announcements.

The duties of the room advisers that are directly concerned with personnel problems are (a) group guidance during the adviser period, (b) interviews with pupils in need of individual guidance and counsel, and (c) visiting each year the homes of all new pupils in the group.

(4) *The director of research.*—The director of research performs a variety of functions, some more closely connected with the adviser-personnel program than others. He is responsible for carrying out the testing program for the entire school. This program includes the giving of group intelligence and achievement tests to the pupils in the high school, the testing of the eighth-grade pupils before they enter high school, and the testing of individual pupils in need of diagnostic study. The director of research is also in charge of the placement work and maintains contacts with positions that are available for the graduates of the high school. In view of the fact that about 90 per cent of the graduates of New Trier Township High School enter higher institutions, the number of pupils to be placed in jobs is never large. As in other high schools at the present time, the activities in regard to vocational placement and follow-up are much restricted.

The most important functions carried on by the director of research in connection with the counseling program is that of conducting special investigations. Although many of the studies reported by the director apply directly to the administrative, instructional, and curriculum problems of the school, a large number of studies are concerned with problems and aspects of the personnel program. These studies relate to the nature and extent of failures, pupil grouping and placement, the nature and extent of problems calling for individual conferences, improvement in scholastic marks as a result of adjustments in personnel problems, etc.

Group guidance.—Group guidance is given to the pupils primarily during the adviser period, a 30-minute period from 8.30 to 9 o'clock every morning excepting Wednesday and Thursday, when the period is used for assembly programs, class meetings, and other class or school activities. The adviser periods are frequently used by the individual adviser for group activities. During this period the daily bulletin is read to the pupils. Routine administrative matters, such as attendance, excuses, programs, assignment of lockers, locker inspection, and other similar duties, are taken care of at this time.

The advisers are expected to use as much of this period as possible for counsel and advice on general problems that apply to all the pupils in the group. Conferences and interviews for individual pupils are arranged for at times other than the adviser-room period. In the freshman year the handbook is used for giving instruction and information concerning the general rules and regulations of the school, tardiness, excuses, absences, library, lunch period, etc. In the classes above the freshman class the period is used for a review of the general rules and regulations of the school and for a consideration of other school and class problems.

Features of the program.—Besides the very complete records maintained for each individual pupil, other features of the adviser-personnel program at New Trier are (a) the guidance and counsel given in respect to the selection of a college and preparation for it and (b) the integration of instructional, administrative, and disciplinary functions with the adviser-personnel organization.

A special feature of the program in this high school is the provision that is made for a group of eighth-grade pupils of low ability. These pupils, numbering about 20, are under the direction of a specially trained and specially interested adviser. The adviser room for this group is removed somewhat from the other adviser rooms, so that the early adjustments of these pupils to the new situations found in high school may progress as rapidly as possible without unpleasant and discouraging contacts with the other pupils of the school. Some of the pupils in this group are retarded because of physical handicaps, and all are poor in English work. Special provisions have been made for the accommodation of the physically handicapped pupils, and an entirely separate class in English, taught by the adviser, has been set up in an effort to help these pupils to improve in reading, use of English, study habits, and general conduct. The plan of the officers in the adviser-personnel program is to place these pupils in regular adviser groups as soon as possible; that is, as soon as satisfactory adjustments have been made in social attitudes, study habits, and scholastic achievement.

Appraisal.—Studies reported by the director of research show that since the present organization for adviser-personnel work has been in operation the number of cases of discipline reported to the deans and principal and the number of failures, especially in the freshman class, have been reduced materially. The special attention given to the problems of adjusting the incoming pupils to the new situation in the high school is claimed to account in a large measure for the reduction in failures in the freshman class.

Because such a large percentage of the graduates of this high school attend college, a large proportion of the problems and activities of the adviser-personnel organization are concerned directly with college selection and entrance. The satisfaction on the part of the graduates in the colleges selected and the success achieved by the graduates in these colleges attest to the effectiveness of the guidance program and organization.

Two distinct problems, however, were brought out in interviews with various officers in the organization: (1) The set-up renders difficult the securing of as many individual pupil conferences as the room advisers and adviser chairmen consider desirable, and (2) the nature of the organization makes difficult the integration of the adviser rooms into class and school units. Another unfavorable comment on the plan arises from the fact that the integration of administrative, instructional, and disciplinary duties with personnel and guidance functions yields a form of organization not generally accepted by authorities in the field of guidance.

Cost of guidance service.—In computing the cost of the guidance program in the New Trier Township High School, only those portions of the salaries which represent actual guidance and counseling duties have been included. On this basis the salary cost of the guidance program in 1931 amounted to $22.22 per pupil. It can not be assumed, however, that if the guidance program were entirely omitted in this high school this cost would be entirely eliminated. Many of the duties performed by the officers in the guidance program would need to be performed even without a formal guidance organization. It is estimated that if the entire program of guidance and counseling were eliminated in this school a saving of about $11 per pupil would be effected. This latter figure, then, more nearly represents the actual cost of the guidance service.

CHAPTER XII : CASE REPORT ON THE THORNTON TOWNSHIP HIGH SCHOOL

General organization.—The staff organization established for personnel and guidance work in the Thornton Township High School, Harvey, Ill., includes (1) the high-school principal, (2) a director of guidance, (3) four class principals, (4) a dean of boys, (5) a dean of girls, and (6) the home-room teachers. Although the lines of authority and responsibility as set up in the organization plan are not always strictly adhered to, the director of guidance, the dean of boys, and the dean of girls are responsible to the principal, the class principals are supervised by the director of guidance, and the home-room teachers are under the direction of the class principals. The organization is not so formal, however, that any pupil, home-room teacher, classroom teacher, or class principal may not have contact directly with the principal of the high school. A diagram illustrating the organization in this school is presented in Figure 19. The solid lines represent the delegation of authority and the broken lines the contacts and cooperative relations.

Duties of officers.—The director of guidance serves as the class principal for the freshman class. He is not responsible for teaching or home-room duties, but distributes his time to coordinating the various aspects of the counseling program for the entire school, directing the work of the other class principals, conducting research studies in instruction and personnel work, and performing the duties of class principal for the freshman class. The class principals are responsible for directing the work of the home-room teachers and interviewing the pupils in their classes. They are relieved of home-room duties and one period a day of regular classroom teaching. The dean of boys and dean of girls have no home-room duties to perform, but have part-time teaching schedules. Their administrative duties are interviewing pupils in need of

[120]

social and moral guidance and directing the work of the two all-school organizations, the boys' club and the girls' club.

The director of guidance as class principal is in charge of the pupils in the freshman class for one year. In the second year these pupils are placed under the sponsorship of a class principal who remains with the group until graduation. Greater effectiveness is claimed for the work of the principals

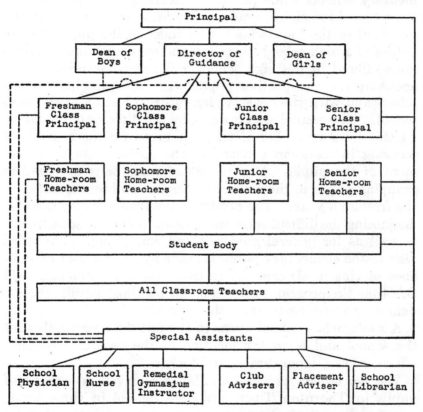

FIGURE 19.—Organization of the guidance program in Thornton Township High School, Harvey, Ill.

if they are permitted to remain in charge of the same group of pupils for three years, and the necessity of making new adjustments between pupils and class principals each year is avoided through this arrangement. The problems of the incoming pupils, however, are unique, and it is felt in this organization that one person who is acquainted with the problems of adjustment peculiar to the first year in high school should perform the duties of guiding and counseling the freshman class each year. Furthermore, the contacts that are to be made by the principal of the freshman class with the eighth-grade pupils before they enter the high school can best be made by the same representative of the school each year rather than by four different representatives.

Preadmission guidance.—Three visits are made to the elementary schools while pupils are nearing the completion of the work of the eighth grade. The first visit is made by the principal of the high school, who talks to the pupils on the values of a high-school education and on the various curriculums offered in the high school. This visit is primarily to acquaint the prospective pupils with the principal of the school and with the general plan of organization of the high school. The second visit is made by the director of guidance. At this time a number of tests are given for the purpose of securing information concerning the aptitude and achievement of the pupils. The results of these tests are used in grouping pupils in the courses in English and mathematics in the freshman year. The results of the tests are also used for diagnosing the difficulties of individuals in need of adjustment, as well as for general guidance and counseling. The third visit to the elementary pupils is made by the director of guidance serving in his capacity as freshman-class principal. At this time the programs are made out for those pupils who are definitely planning to enter the high school.

A week before school opens in the fall the new pupils visit the school and learn the location of the various buildings, offices, rooms, laboratories, and lockers.

The home-room period.—Guidance is given to groups of pupils in Thornton Township High School in three ways, namely, through the home-room period, the vocational-civics course, and the boys' and girls' clubs. During the home-room period of 20 minutes held at the opening of school each day, direct instruction is given to the pupils concerning the problems they are likely to meet in their scholastic careers. In the freshman year instruction is given in the use of the "T" book, the school handbook, on the following points: (*a*) General rules and regulations of the school; (*b*) general conduct in corridors, cafeteria, assembly, library, and classrooms; (*c*) care of school property, and attitude toward teachers, principals, and assembly programs; (*d*) the marking system and the meaning of the various marks; (*e*) absence and tardiness; (*f*) curriculums; (*g*) honors and honor rolls; (*h*) study habits; and (*i*) character development. Above the freshman year the 20-minute home-room period is devoted to a review of the "T" book and, in addition, to instruction in self-analysis, vocational information, manners, and right conduct in the school. A group of small handbooks prepared by the principal is used for this instruction.

Vocational civics course.—All pupils in the first year are required to take a course in vocational civics in which instruction is given concerning occupations and the problems connected with a wise choice of a life vocation.

Boys' and girls' clubs.—All pupils in the school automatically become members of these two organizations through membership in the school. Direct instruction is given by the sponsors of the clubs, the dean of boys or the dean of girls, through a definite program of informal talks, demonstrations, and discussions. These clubs exert a strong influence on the student body in shaping opinions and attitudes toward the social and moral problems that usually arise in high schools.

Individual counseling.—Pupils in need of individual counseling are identified in three ways:

(1) Classroom or home-room teachers who know that pupils are failing in courses or are experiencing other forms of difficulty may suggest to the pupils that they visit their class principals. These teachers also may inform the class principals of the pupils' difficulties, the class principals then calling the pupils for individual conferences.

(2) Pupils may voluntarily come to the class principals for conferences in regard to any problem that may confront them.

(3) Class principals, through an examination of records and reports filed in the central office, may learn of the need on the part of pupils for conferences. These pupils may then be summoned by the class principals for interviews.

Although the largest number of individual interviews come as a result of the class principals' requesting pupils to come to their office, many pupils seek interviews of their own accord. The practices of class principals differ widely, the variations depending on the personality, sympathy, and friendliness of these officers.

Interviews.—Interviews are held with each pupil at least once a year. At this time the pupil's program for the next year is made out. The number of interviews varies, depending both on pupils and the class principals. Pupils who experience difficulty in making adjustments socially or scholastically may have a number of interviews until adjustments are satisfactorily made; pupils who are outstanding and are achieving honors either scholastically or in extra-curriculum activities may also have a number of contacts with the principals; but pupils who are neither outstanding nor problem cases will very likely have few personal interviews with their class principals.

Individual conferences are held in an office that has been set aside for the class principals of the sophomore, junior, and senior classes. The principal of the freshman class has a private office. It might be more desirable if each principal had a private office. However, the office hours are arranged as much as possible at different periods in the day, so that in actual practice the work of each principal is not materially embarrassed by lack of privacy.

The technique employed in the interviews varies with the principals, the pupils, and the nature of the problem. In general, an effort is made to bring the following points to the attention of both the pupils and the class principals: (*a*) A clear understanding of the problem before the pupil, (*b*) the relation of the problem to the life and scholastic career of the pupil, (*c*) the relation of the problem of the individual pupil to the general school society, (*d*) the instruction and information that the pupil may have received in the home-room period or the boys' or girls' club concerning the type of problem, and (*e*) the proper or desirable procedure to be followed in effective adjustment.

Records.—Extensive and detailed records for guidance and counseling are not maintained at Thornton Township High School. Effective contacts are had between class prin-'cipals and pupils with the records that are kept, however. The feeling has been expressed by class principals, the director of guidance, and the principal of the high school that the contact with the pupil in need of counseling and the results of that contact as expressed in the conduct and attitude of the pupil are more important factors in a guidance program than extensive and detailed reports and records. Many personal letters are sent to the parents of pupils concerning any problems that arise. Copies of these letters are kept in the office of the class principals and serve as the main source of records and reports of the personnel work. Complete scholastic records are also maintained in this office, as well as a small card for each pupil on which various items of information are recorded from time to time.

Vocational guidance and placement.—Guidance in vocational choices is given largely through the freshman course on vocational civics and in the home rooms. The class principals, however, supplement this instruction with individual conferences whenever necessary. The director of guidance serves as chairman of a committee on vocational placement, but during the last few years little has been done in this work owing to the small demand for high-school graduates in vocations.

Appraisal of the guidance program.—Numerous studies have been made by the director of guidance in regard to the effectiveness of the program. These studies have indicated a greatly reduced number of pupil failures and withdrawals and an increased number of satisfactory adjustments on the part of pupils. The program has proved effective especially in eliminating unnecessary delay in putting into operation the regular schedule of classes on the opening day of school. Because of the work done with the eighth-grade pupils in the elementary schools and with the freshmen, sophomores, and juniors in the high school in the months just preceding the summer vacation, registration for classes for the following year is completed before the opening of school in the fall. Only the first two periods of the first day of school are taken up with routine administrative matters on opening day, and regular classes are under way at the third period of that day.

The effectiveness of the guidance program, furthermore, is evident through the success of the direct methods of instruction given both in the 20-minute home-room periods and in the boys' and girls' clubs. The results of this training are evident in the conduct and attitudes of the pupils in all parts of the school. The program of guidance and counseling has influenced the school morale in a decided manner. This improvement has been noted by visitors, teachers, and pupils, and was illustrated in a definite manner to the writer of this report through interviews with several of the high-school pupils.

Cost of guidance service.—From data reported by the superintendent of the Thornton Township High School it was found that an average of $2.68 per pupil is being expended in this school for the guidance services provided for the 1,700 pupils enrolled. In computing this cost, only the portions of the salaries of the dean of boys, dean of girls, class principals, and the director of guidance which represent duties performed in connection with the guidance program are included. These officers perform other duties in the school which are not directly connected with the organized guidance service but which would have to be performed even if no guidance program were provided. The cost figure, then, applies only to the duties and functions performed by these officers in carrying out the organized guidance service.

CHAPTER XIII : CASE REPORT ON THE LA SALLE-PERU TOWNSHIP HIGH SCHOOL

Organization and purpose.—The Bureau of Educational Counsel of the La Salle-Peru Township High School was established in September, 1923. The organization was made possible as a result of a mental health survey of the district composed of the three cities, La Salle, Peru, and Oglesby, by the Institute of Juvenile Research of Chicago in the spring of 1923, and a generous annual grant to the board of education of the township high school by a public-spirited citizen of La Salle for the support of the bureau.

The purposes of the bureau, as stated by the late superintendent of the school, are:

to study intensively the individual needs of high-school pupils; to estimate their native abilities and disabilities; to discover their occupational bents and aspirations; to plan their school courses; to indicate the careers and vocations they may reasonably follow; and to remove the main obstacles to these ends by a sympathetic study of their behavior type, personality, environment, history, and emotional mechanisms.[1]

The services of the bureau were extended in 1925 to the junior college [2] which had been established in connection with the high school in 1924, the request coming from the students who appreciated the benefits derived from contacts with the personnel of the bureau while they were pupils in the high school.

The relation of the bureau to the school and the methods of its functioning are shown in Figure 20. All pupils are reached directly by the bureau through personal interviews, general talks, and psychological tests. Certain individuals

---

[1] McCormack, T. J. The Bureau of Educational Counsel, p. 1. Report for 1923–1926, La Salle, Ill.

[2] For a discussion of the guidance services in the junior college see article by Lila McNutt: Psychiatric Social Work in the La Salle-Peru-Oglesby Junior College. Mental Hygiene, 13: 271–277, April, 1929.

may receive follow-up service on request of principal, teachers, or parents.

Composition of the pupil personnel.—The school has an enrollment of approximately 1,500 pupils, 1,250 in grades 9 to 12 and 250 in the junior college. The pupils come from underlying elementary-school districts and parochial schools, since the high school and junior college is of the independent

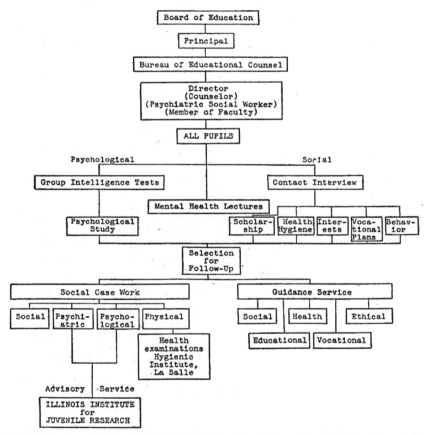

FIGURE 20.—Organization of the Bureau of Educational Counsel, La Salle-Peru Township High School and La Salle-Peru-Oglesby Junior College

township organization. A disadvantage of this type of organization is lack of articulation between the lower schools and the secondary school. Pupils are received from 9 parochial schools, 5 city elementary schools, and 20 rural schools. The freshman class numbers about 450. Of this number, 350 enter in the fall and 100 at the middle of the school year. The boys usually outnumber the girls in the freshman class.

The community is industrial and agricultural, and the majority of the pupils come from wage-earning groups. A large percentage of the parents in the wage-earning groups are foreign born.

Personnel of the bureau.—The personnel of the bureau consists of a director and two assistants, all of whom are trained psychiatric social workers, and one clerk, who acts as secretary. The director and the two assistants are designated as counselors, and their chief service to the pupils is counseling.

Two counselors and the secretary are employed for the calendar year. They spend the summer months on social case work, on the organization of the record materials, and in carrying on research. The director and two assistants have the rank of teachers on the faculty of the school. The director is considered one of the administrative officers of the school.

Information collected by the bureau.—When a pupil is admitted to the school, the secretary of the bureau prepares a record (face sheet) for the individual, consisting of date and place of birth; sex; grade; course; schools previously attended, with grades and marks in each; grades repeated or skipped; and participation in school activities. The names of the parents and their nationality, religion, occupation, and the language spoken in the home are recorded, and names of other children, with ages, schools attended, and occupations, if employed, are also included. A psychological test is subsequently given by a psychologist from the Institute for Juvenile Research, Chicago, Ill., and record is made of mental age, intelligence quotient, and test score. Achievement tests in arithmetic, reading, language usage, and literature are also given and record made of the grade placement, grade age, and test score.

A cumulative folder is kept for each pupil in which are filed the interview material; that is, a summary of his school history, health history, hygiene interest scope and plans for the future, the personality ratings made by the teachers, report of the medical examination of the pupil, achievement and psychological rating, vocational record, and correspondence and other memorandums regarding the pupil.

The information secured is correlated and evaluated by the counselor and is used as a basis for further case work if the findings indicate such need; as, for instance, when the individual seeks advice from the counselor or is referred to the counselor by principal or teacher.

Group guidance.—Group talks on aspects of mental health are given by the director of the bureau during the school year. A general talk is given to the freshmen early in the fall, and two talks on mental hygiene to freshmen and sophomores each year. The approach is made through the subjects of personality and behavior. Occasionally an entire class period may be devoted to the discussion of some trait, such as "excuse-forming" or "day-dreaming." Talks to seniors are given once a year. Occasional talks on mental health are given by the visiting psychiatrist to groups of pupils. Talks on vocations by representatives of business or professions are considered usually of little value and are not encouraged.

Individual guidance.—Guidance by psychiatric social workers is largely an individual matter. Each pupil is regarded as an individual case to be studied and treated with respect to his behavior in life. Through conferences with individuals the counselors seek to aid the pupils in self-discovery and adjustment. The materials previously described form the basis for the approach.

Various aspects of guidance are considered with the pupils, such as educational, vocational, social, ethical, and health. While some aspect of guidance may be more prominent in a given case than the others, the tendency of the counselor is to regard all aspects as closely related and directed to the same end, namely, the development of human personality.

The school accomplishment of the pupils is studied in relation to capacity, and counsel is given regarding the choice of courses and subjects. Failing pupils are interviewed, and an attempt is made to diagnose the causes and to advise both pupils and teachers regarding corrective and remedial measures. Successful pupils are also studied and are encouraged to develop their special abilities.

Direct vocational guidance is offered only in the case of pupils leaving school by withdrawal or graduation. The view of the psychiatric social worker is that determining the vocational choice of a pupil is not the responsibility of the school. The counselor, therefore, seeks to develop an insight into abilities and temperament in relation to vocations, leaving the choice of occupation to the pupil.

Through the personal interview with the pupil the counselor aids the pupil in making adjustments to his social environment, in overcoming physical and health handicaps, and in giving guidance with respect to personality traits and emotional habits.

The more common phases of personal guidance [3] attempted by the counselors are:

(1) Developing the self-conscious, inadequate personality whose feelings of inferiority may or may not have a real basis.

(2) Reducing egocentric tendencies in the student whose self-estimate is too high.

(3) Stimulating to greater action the day dreamer, who is rich in vision but poor in genuine achievement.

(4) Broadening the childish immature personality from unreasonable excuse-forming tendencies.

(5) Widening the interest scope of the narrow individual unresponsive to stimuli and inflexible in reaction.

(6) Substituting adequate compensations for unsatisfactory defense mechanisms.

(7) In general, attacking the unhealthy personality traits and undesirable emotional habits that they may be replaced by more favorable ones.

Psychiatric clinics.—Monthly clinics of two or three days' duration are held by the Institute for Juvenile Research, Chicago, for pupils in need of mental health service. The clinical staff consists of a psychologist and a psychiatrist. Appointments are made for the pupils in advance, and generally seven or eight are examined. The superior pupil whose achievement in school is not commensurate with his capacity is the type favored for clinical study. However, the clinics are not limited to this type. Any pupil who may profit by contact with the psychiatrist, either for corrective or for enrichment purposes, is given the opportunity to see him. Be-

[3] Olson, Elma. The Bureau of Educational Counsel, p. 35. Report for 1923–1926, La Salle, Ill.

cause of limitations of time it is a selective matter depending largely on the judgment of the counselor.

Services of Hygienic Institute.—The Hygienic Institute of La Salle, serving La Salle, Peru, and Oglesby, is a chartered institution endowed by a public-spirited and philanthropic citizen of La Salle for the purpose of protecting the health of the people of these communities and for carrying on scientific research, particularly in the field of preventive medicine. The institute is housed in property of the board of education on the school grounds.

Physical examination of all new pupils entering the high school is made at the beginning of each school year by a health officer of the institute and recommendations are made for their health guidance. When medical service is required the pupil is referred to his family physician for treatment. Medical follow-up is done subsequently to the interview with the counselor, so that other information gathered may be utilized, if desired, in the treatment. Pupils with health problems are given precedence to this end in scheduling interviews. If a pupil proves to have only a health problem with no social complications, he may be referred to a nurse of the Hygienic Institute for follow-up. If special arrangements must be made, the counselor carries the medical problem also to prevent duplication of visits in the home or doctor's office. The Hygienic Institute serves the Bureau of Educational Counsel in an advisory capacity in health cases. It may render first-aid treatment in special cases of injury at the school.

The close affiliation of the Hygienic Institute with the Bureau of Educational Counsel makes possible the utilization by the bureau of the physical records and medical services of the institute in the guidance of pupils. The medical records are kept in the files in the bureau office.

Tri-Cities Family Welfare Society.—The Bureau of Educational Counsel can secure the cooperation of the Tri-Cities Family Welfare Society in special cases. This society carries on family welfare service in the communities, stressing family case work and relief. The counselor represents the pupil when plans involving a family's welfare are being considered by the welfare society. The Bureau of Educational

Counsel is thus able to deal effectively with environmental influences which affect the personality of the pupil and his progress in school.

High-school and community social center.—A school and community recreational and social center is maintained in a building adjacent to the high school with a staff of trained workers who are members of the high-school faculty. The activities of the social center are social and athletic, consisting of dances, parties, clubs, and competitive games and sports. The counselor is able to render both social and physical guidance to individual pupils through her relation to the social-center staff.

Placement service.—Cooperative relations are maintained between the counselors and the personnel departments of the industries which employ the graduates of the high school. Aptitude tests are administered by the counselors to pupils who indicate a desire to seek employment in local industries, and the results are reported to the personnel officers of the industries. Visits between officers to discuss problems of placement are frequent. Part-time placements are made for pupils who need to earn while attending school.

Unique features of the plan.—The work of the Bureau of Educational Counsel is similar in many respects to the activities of guidance organizations in other schools. It differs from other plans chiefly in the following respects:

(1) The approach of the counselor is through the principles of mental hygiene. The technique employed is that of the psychiatric social worker. Each pupil is studied as a case, the emphasis being placed on behavior, the development of personality, and the adjustment of emotional conflicts common to adolescent life.

(2) Pupils desiring or requiring expert advice are provided for in monthly psychiatric clinics conducted by staff members of the Institute for Juvenile Research.

(3) An unusual organization for institutional cooperation has been effected in the communities comprising this secondary-school district which makes possible types of guidance frequently rendered impossible by counselors in other schools.

(4) Although the program definitely provides guidance services for all pupils, the emphasis is placed on the fullest development of the superior pupil.

(5) The program places the responsibility for taking the initiative in guidance on the counselor, although initiative by pupils, parents, and teachers is encouraged. Initiative in guidance by the counselor may be taken in two ways: (*a*) The Bureau of Educational Counsel takes initiative for its program in the school setting, that is, planning the psychological tests, achievement tests, the more particularized medical examination than is usually made for physical-culture purposes, procuring the face-sheet information, and sending out personality blanks for the ratings (opinions) of teachers, all aiming at the consideration of the specific or individual pupil, though done in mass attack. All entering pupils are routinely scheduled for interview by the counselor. (*b*) If this correlated information shows discrepancies in wholesome living conditions or healthy personality development as judged by the counselor trained in this work, she takes the initiative in evaluating its effect on the pupil in making adjustments which will tend to correct the condition. It is this initiative which the pupil, parent, teacher, or family physician may take in bringing to the attention of the counselor the specific need of a given pupil.

(6) The service extends from the ninth grade through the junior college. In the latter institution the service was initiated at the request of the students.

Cost of the service.—The cost of the guidance service is approximately $8,500 per year, or a per pupil cost of $5.66. Of this amount, $7,000 is provided annually as a gift by a public-spirited citizen, leaving $1,500, or about $1 per pupil, as the actual annual cost to the school.

CHAPTER XIV : AN OVERVIEW OF GUIDANCE PROGRAMS

The four types of programs.—The foregoing case reports disclose four general types of guidance programs: (1) Centralized bureaus of guidance for secondary schools in city systems, represented by Boston, Chicago, and Cincinnati; (2) city school systems with a central guidance organization but with the individual secondary school considered the unit in the program, represented by Providence and Milwaukee; (3) centralized bureaus or departments in individual secondary schools, represented by the Milwaukee Vocational School and the Township High School and Junior College, La Salle, Ill.; (4) central guidance organizations in individual secondary schools which utilize regular officers and teachers as guidance functionaries, represented by the Joliet Township High School and Junior College, the Thornton Township High School, and the New Trier Township High School. Virtually the same guidance activities are undertaken under the different programs. The chief variations consist in the methods employed in the several school systems and individual schools and some difference in emphasis on certain phases of guidance activity, such as vocational guidance, educational guidance, or psychiatric social guidance.

1. *The central guidance bureau in city school systems.*— Principles formulated by the National Vocational Guidance Association [1] in 1921, and revised in 1924, 1930, and 1931, urge the development of a special bureau or separate departments responsible directly to the superintendent of schools for carrying on vocational guidance service. While recognizing the fact that local conditions render impossible the prescription of the exact form of the bureau or department, the activities to be performed are specified and the recommendation made that the activities be performed only by persons possessing the necessary personal qualifications, experience, and training. Obviously, the plan was intended

[1] See Basic Units for an Introductory Course in Vocational Guidance, pp. 181-194. McGraw-Hill Book Co. (Inc.), 1931.

for use in school systems and individual schools of considerable size.

The organization of a guidance bureau makes possible the carrying on of certain guidance activities, such as occupational research, follow-up studies, and vocational guidance in connection with placement in a central office apart from the administrative work of the schools. A staff of trained workers can be maintained who not only perform the office duties incident to guidance but who also visit schools on call and engage in group instruction, group counseling, and individual counseling. They may also give advice to teachers, parents, and administrative officers regarding guidance of an unspecialized sort that can be carried on in the schools or homes by persons not specifically trained for guidance work.

The director of the guidance bureau is usually responsible to an assistant superintendent or to the superintendent. The director is expected to formulate the guidance policy of the school system subject to the approval of his superior officers; to organize the bureau or department as a clearing house for problems of guidance, placement, and follow-up; and to provide assistants who can render expert counseling service to schools desiring such aid.

The activities which can be carried on in the schools by the guidance assistants are: Group interviewing of pupils in entering classes, individual interviewing of members of the graduating class, individual interviewing of pupils as needs arise, instructing classes in occupations, assisting graduates or pupils required to leave school to secure employment, keeping records of pupils interviewed, visiting employers to enlist their interests and to secure knowledge of the conditions under which employed pupils work, conducting community surveys to ascertain environmental conditions and opportunities for employment, and carrying on follow-up studies of withdrawals and graduates.

The guidance bureau is not expected to provide all the guidance service in the individual schools of the system. The principal of each individual school, through his teachers and administrative assistants, is expected to aid pupils in the choice of courses or subjects, in the selection of extra-curriculum activities, in the development of intellectual interests, in social adjustments, in overcoming difficulties in classroom work, and the like. The guidance bureau provides the specialized service and aids the principal in the organization of the school's guidance program and in the integration of its various guidance activities.

In large cities the staff of the guidance bureau is usually inadequate to provide all the guidance service needed in all the schools.[2] Some schools of a system will be satisfied with nominal services, while others will desire all the service possible for the bureau to render. As a result, the guidance programs in the individual schools of a school system often vary greatly in both scope and effectiveness. This condition is largely chargeable to the administrators of the individual schools rather than to the central bureau.

The development of the central bureau of guidance in school systems and in large schools makes possible occupational research and the utilization of the findings in vocational guidance and placement to an extent scarcely possible under the other types of programs. However, the guidance activities that belong in the individual schools are likely to be neglected unless complementary guidance programs are developed by the principals of the schools or are projected by the guidance-bureau for individual schools. The weakness of the guidance programs under the control of central bureaus is not inherent, but rather the result of the objectives of the bureaus.

2. *The central guidance organization in a city system with the individual secondary school the unit.*—This type of guidance organization places the responsibility for the guidance program on the head of the individual secondary school. A central organization is established to render consultant service to the principals and specialized services to the local guidance functionaries. The plan eliminates the necessity of specific appropriations in the budget solely for guidance purposes. Guidance is integrated with education and is supported as a vital part of the work of the individual school. The activities of guidance should be differentiated and definitely assigned to officers of administration and teachers properly qualified to carry on the activities assigned.

---

[2] For example, in 1930–31 Chicago had a staff of 31; Boston, 18; and Cincinnati, 8.

The administrative officers, consisting of principal, vice principal, deans, director of extracurriculum activities, and department heads, accept executive responsibility for providing the program of studies, materials of instruction, the record system; admission of pupils to school; classification of pupils; preparation of the school schedule; arrangement of the program of pupil activities; and administration of cases of discipline. They interview parents; administer attendance; record and evaluate credits; and organize, direct, and supervise the functioning of the different members of the school staff. Many of the activities of the administrative officers affect guidance only indirectly; yet unless the relation of administrative activities to guidance is clearly conceived the guidance activities of other workers may be hampered or completely inhibited.

The director of guidance in any individual school, in case there is such an official, projects the guidance program subject to the approval of the head of the school. He outlines the guidance activities to be performed by the counselors, home-room advisers, and teachers and provides the training needed to carry on the guidance program. He interprets the guidance program to the school and community, carries on research basic to guidance, and performs guidance activities which require types of skill not possessed by the other members of the staff.

The counselors teach the courses in occupations, aid the pupils in the selection of courses, give group guidance to all the pupils, and counsel with individual pupils in need of adjustment. They may also serve part time as regular teachers.

The home-room advisers may accept responsibility for the orientation of their pupils, the maintenance of pupil morale, and the development of a wholesome attitude toward the school as a civic enterprise. The advisers keep the records of the pupils, give advice with respect to extracurriculum and other social activities, and act as intermediaries for the pupils with administrative and guidance officers and parents.

The teacher must be encouraged to play a large part in the guidance program of the individual school. His interest in the welfare of the pupil is indispensable, if guidance is to bear fruit. He should sense the symptoms of maladjustment in a pupil in the incipient stages, bring the guidance organization to bear on the case, contribute to the diagnosis of the causes of maladjustment, and assist in the application of the corrective or remedial measures advised. Furthermore, the teacher may give specific guidance to pupils in the pursuit of intellectual interests, in the development of proper habits of study, and in the development of the proper conception of the processes of education and the opportunities for education provided through the school.

The foregoing analysis of the activities of the guidance functionaries offers promise of a balanced program of counseling and guidance for the individual secondary schools of a city system. The neglect of any of the important phases of guidance, either through failure to give them proper emphasis or through failure to assign them to the proper guidance officers for performance, may contribute to maladjustment and failure of pupils.

The central organization is responsible for encouraging the development of complete programs of guidance in the individual secondary schools. The chief official of the central organization may be an executive officer, as in the case of Providence, R. I., or a consulting officer, as in the case of Milwaukee, Wis. In either case he is likely to function in the individual school as an adviser to the principal and an instructor for the other administrative officers and teachers. Through supervision he seeks to develop a guidance program in all of the individual schools in accordance with the guidance policy of the central organization.

Guidance service on a State basis of the type under consideration was proposed at the meeting of the National Vocational Guidance Association, February 21, 1930. A committee on State guidance programs and activities was appointed, which, in conjunction with a National Advisory Committee, submitted a preliminary report at the meeting of the association in 1931 offering suggestions for the organization of State guidance programs. Thirty-nine States, according to the report of the committee, have appointed representatives to cooperate with the National Vocational Guidance Association and the National Advisory Committee.

Nine of these States have launched guidance programs. The committee believes that the appointment of a full-time, trained guidance director, supervisor, specialist, or counselor for a school, district, county, or State is greatly to be desired, although not essential at the start. It is often possible to find some one in the State department who is willing to accept the responsibility for the promotion of guidance work on a part-time basis. The county program is regarded by the committee as one of the most effective devices for developing a state-wide guidance service. The county superintendent of schools is able through his office to reach all principals of a county, whether the schools are under his supervision or not. The county guidance officer is thus able to reach the smaller secondary schools and can give direction and encouragement in the development of guidance programs for the local schools. The State guidance service may be placed under a guidance director or some other member of the State department who can cooperate with the county officer in holding conferences and in distributing guidance material prepared by the State department. The material may be in the form of a syllabus or textbook. The important function of a State guidance service is the development of guidance programs in the small secondary schools.

The plan under consideration seeks to develop a complete, functioning, supervised program, rather than a divided program with certain guidance activities carried on by specialists in the central bureau and other activities carried on by specialists in the individual schools. In contrast with the central bureau type, this plan looks toward developing guidance service in every school, not only in those where the leadership seeks the guidance service of the central bureau and for which a limited service is available.

3. *Centralized guidance organization in individual schools.*— In secondary schools in which the principal is the chief executive officer, with full power or much autonomy to organize and administer his school, a guidance organization may be effected very similar in character to that of the central bureau type in city systems. The guidance organization can be made a structural part of the school organization and func-

tional responsibility delegated to the director for organizing and carrying on the guidance activities specified in the school program. The director and his staff may undertake to carry on all guidance activities or he may organize his department to carry on certain activities and delegate to administrative officers and teachers certain other activities retaining supervisory oversight. In either case the possibility of coordinating the guidance activities of the individual school is greater than under the central bureau type of organization for a city system.

The programs of the two schools[3] for which case reports have been presented vary markedly in character, although the type of organization is much the same. Guidance is a department in the administrative organization of each school, and the directors are executive officers of their departments with executive authority in carrying on the guidance functions of the school. They may summon individual pupils for conference, administer tests to classes or groups, give advice to pupils regarding the choice of college or occupation, make contacts with business organizations and industry with respect to placements, carry on research investigations designed to facilitate guidance, and cooperate with welfare organizations in the interests of the pupil personnel of the school.

The central organization in the individual school has a distinct advantage over its prototype, the central bureau of the city systems, in that its activities are concentrated instead of dissipated among a number of schools. In operation it more closely resembles the guidance organizations in city systems which emphasize the individual schools as units; it differs from them by maintaining a staff of guidance officers instead of utilizing regular administrative officers and teachers.

4. *Central guidance organizations in individual schools utilizing regular officers and teachers as functionaries.*—In schools[4] classified under this type of guidance organization the principal or a trained counselor serves as director of the

---

[3] Milwaukee Vocational School and Township High School and Junior College, La Salle, Ill.
[4] Joliet Township High School and Junior College, Thornton Township High School, and New Trier Township High School.

guidance program. Administrative officers and teachers are utilized as functionaries in carrying on guidance activities.

Large secondary schools with large staffs of officers and teachers make possible the selection of functionaries with special aptitude or training for guidance duties and the differentiation of duties along functional lines. The prevailing organization of the guidance work in the large schools is the home-room plan supplemented by special administrative officers, such as the dean of girls, dean of boys, director of personnel, director of extracurriculum activities, and the like, or class principals, advisory committees, and special counselors.

Through functionaries of the kinds indicated pupils are guided in their choice of curriculums, the adjustment of their schedules, the selection of extracurriculum activities, the correction of disabilities, the development of special interests and abilities, the choice of a college or occupation, and in securing placement. Activities of the sort specified are closely related. Unless the school organizes and coordinates the work of the functionaries who perform the activities into a program the guidance services will likely be haphazard and unsystematic.

The data available and the cases reported show great variation in the guidance programs of the large secondary schools. In some schools the guidance duties are assumed chiefly by home-room advisers; in others, by special officers, such as class principals and committees; in others, by administrative officers.

It is scarcely possible for the small secondary school to secure either the full-time or the part-time service of a trained worker in the field of guidance. Its program of guidance must therefore be developed by the principal and carried on either by him or his teachers.[5]

An example of this type of guidance program is reported by Proctor [6] for a small rural high school in California. The principal of this high school has developed a program for his school which consists of a number of elements.

[5] See sec. 3 of ch. IX, Pupil Accounting and Guidance, in Monograph No. 6 of the National Survey of Secondary Education.

[6] Ibid., pp. 14–16.

(1) The plan includes a visiting day for the eighth-grade graduates who are to enter the high school the following semester. The graduates spend a day at the high school as the guests of the teachers and student body. They are shown through the building, are given information regarding the program of study and the work of the different departments, and are entertained at a dinner by the high-school pupils. (2) The high-school principal visits the elementary schools and secures an individual record of each pupil who is to enter the high school the following semester. The record includes scholastic marks of the pupil, the results of mental and achievement tests in the elementary-school subjects, and confidential information regarding the personal history and qualifications of the pupil. (3) During the month prior to the opening of school the principal or the freshman-class adviser visits the homes of all the prospective freshmen. Notice of the visit is sent in advance, and a conference is arranged with the parents and pupil to discuss the plans of the pupil for his first year in the high school. (4) A registration day on Friday or Saturday preceding the opening is held at the school. The pupils come with their parents for a conference with the principal and class adviser. At this conference a tentative schedule for each pupil is prepared and formal registration takes place. (5) Pupils are grouped in ability sections in English and in mathematics. (6) The class adviser continues with the freshmen as adviser until they graduate from the school. (7) The class adviser keeps a record of the pupils and counsels with them regarding their school progress. (8) A 6-weeks unit in the civics course for seniors is given over to vocational information. (9) The teachers in charge of physical education for boys and girls have the county school nurse give advice on social, moral, and health problems. (10) The work of the guidance program is carefully supervised by the principal and the work of the different persons responsible for guidance is articulated through the principal.

In either large or small schools a guidance program may be developed for an individual school as an integral part of the educational program. The cost of the program may be either greater or less than that of the central guidance department in individual secondary schools, depending on the elaborateness of the organization and the utilization of the administrative or teaching personnel for separate guidance activites. The evidence indicates that the cost of the guidance program will be less if regular officers and teachers are utilized as guidance functionaries.

CPSIA information can be obtained
at www.ICGtesting.com
Printed in the USA
BVHW071119080119
537312BV00021B/684/P